THE LORD IS MY SHEPHERD

The Lord Is My Shepherd

Witnesses of Priests

Collected by:
George W. Kosicki, C.S.B.

**"The Lord is my shepherd;
I shall not want."**

Psalm 23

Copyright ©1973 Servant Publications

Published by: Servant Books
Box 8617
Ann Arbor, Michigan 48107

Available From: Servant Publications
Distribution Center
237 North Michigan
South Bend, Indiana 46601

Book Design by Unfolding His Word.
Cover sculpture by Fr. Bohdan Kosicki

Fr. Matt Killian's testimony reprinted from *Voice,* April 1970
courtesy of Full Gospel Business Men's Fellowship International,
836 South Figueroa Street, Los Angeles, California 90017

ISBN 0-89283-006-9

Contents

Contents

To My Brother Priests:

Faith comes from hearing; when we hear of the faith of a brother our own faith is built up. The reason we share our spiritual journey is not that anyone should follow in the same footsteps, but that others might recognize God's action in their own lives. When I hear the story of God's ways in my brother, I can recognize the Lord's touch in myself. I can say, "Yes. That is what he is doing in me."

These witnesses to God's action have been written with the sincere hope that they will move our brother priests as much as they have moved each of us. The Church and the world need men who are touched by God and can recognize that touch in themselves and others. We need men who are moved by God and can respond to that movement with discernment and free response. We need men who want to, and can, respond to God and the proclamation of his kingdom with their whole being.

God has touched each of these men in a unique way. I have known each of these men (with the exception of Fr. Matt Killian) and have known what power has been released in their lives. These men and many others like them are the beginning of a "Spiritual Revolution" in the Church. It only takes a handful of totally committed men to turn the direction of the times. The power for this Spiritual Revolution is without limit. It is the same power at work in us that raised Jesus from the dead (Eph. 1).

In my travels through South and Central America, North America, and the Orient giving renewal retreats to priests, I have come to realize the importance of reaching out to my fellow priests. When one priest is renewed by the power of the Holy Spirit he in turn reaches out to many thousands of people. The intention of this collection of witnesses of God's work in priests is that more priests will respond unconditionally to the call of the Lord and the work of the kingdom. When the shepherds are renewed then the sheep can expect fresh nourishment and guidance.

How uniquely God touched each of these men is expressed in their own stories. Even the style and language reflect their uniqueness. I want to extend my thanks to my brothers for their efforts in writing their stories. May their thanks be expressed in your grateful pondering of God's marvels in their hearts.

In Christ Jesus,
George W. Kosicki, CSB
June 21, 1973

Fr. Timothy Nolan / 1

Rev. Timothy Nolan was ordained in the Archdiocese of Minneapolis-St. Paul in 1967. He works as a counselor on the formation staff of St. John Vianney Seminary in St. Paul, Minnesota, and is a coordinator of the St. Paul the Apostle Charismatic Community.

Fr. Timothy Nolan

I have always envisioned priests as having a very special relationship with God. They must enjoy his presence continually, walking with him each morning as Adam did in the cool of the garden dusk. How great must be the power they experience as God's mercy and love, healing, and salvation flow through them to God's people.

The seminary and first years of priesthood had occasional moments that approached that vision, but by and large were disappointing. God seemed very distant and formal, approached mostly through hard acts of faith which brought only the satisfaction that comes when a difficult job has been completed and you can look back with a feeling of accomplishment.

In the first months and years following ordination in 1967, it seemed God had played a trick on me. Those were the days of a great exodus from priesthood. As I was breaking into priesthood, many were breaking out; as I was reaching out toward that vision of a full life in the ministry, many were withdrawing. It was as if they had tried it, some for years, and found it wanting. What was I to think?

As experiences accumulated and the novelty of those first Masses, confessions, Communions, weddings, funerals, convert instructions, counseling sessions, etc., wore off, the quality and kind of my commitment began to be seriously challenged. I was assigned to the formation staff in our archdiocesan college seminary, and found the challenge increased. There seemed to be a constant pressure to be an example and witness to the priestly ideal, to somehow bridge the gap between the vision of my youth and the reality I had experienced in priesthood. More and more, I began to feel like a hypocrite. I dreaded preaching. I felt like I had nothing to say and what I did say seemed hollow. I was becoming more and more disillusioned as I recognized the politics and human weakness that seemed to permeate the local church. There seemed to be a noticeable lack of any direct influence by God. He was seldom referred to except in formal prayers and liturgy. Most of the problems, decisions, and directives of the Church seemed largely to involve human wisdom fraught with human weakness. Spiritual support from brother priests, religious, and laymen seemed nonexistent or, if extant, so tightly guarded it was never suspected. Yet the demands and requests for service continued to increase far beyond any realistic expectations. The suspicion began to arise somewhere in the back roads of my mind that priesthood was a holding action, a housekeeping maintenance function that tried to keep a dying, largely ineffectual organization from extinction.

Prayer had become non-communication and was only attempted in the ritual formulas of liturgy. Private prayer and meditation were forgotten experiences and the occasional efforts to read the office were discouraging gestures issuing in questions like: "What does it all mean?" "Why?" "For what?" With each addition to the list of priests leaving, the anguish increased and the questions intensified. The growing pain brought new efforts to escape into self-indulgence and self-pity.

The undaunted enthusiasm of the seminarians that I lived and worked with seemed so naive. Did they really know what they were getting into?

With the departure from priesthood of two of my close friends and classmates, the question began to arise more forcefully and clearly: "Why should I stay in the ministry? What were they seeing that I wasn't seeing? Were they crazy to leave or was I crazy to stay?" The question bounced back and forth off the walls of my mind, and I began to entertain the possibility of leaving the active ministry. Almost by way of the last straw or push on the edge of a cliff, news came about the priest I had idolized most. He had been my inspiration to enter the priesthood, was a source of encouragement and support during my seminary years, and had preached at my first Mass. Word came that he was leaving the active ministry after years of remarkable success and brilliant service as a priest.

My discouragement and disillusionment seemed complete and a new reaction welled up in me. I actually began to fear that I might leave the ministry and at the same time recognized down deep inside that I really didn't want to leave.

Then I remembered a conversation I had had with my sister a year before. She had made a Cursillo and was really excited about it and strongly recommended that I make one. My response was: "I'll keep it until I need it," and I didn't think I needed it then.

Well if I would ever need it, now was the time. When a phone call came inviting me to make a Cursillo weekend, I said yes and decided it would be a last ditch effort toward survival. That weekend ignited a flickering flame of hope which was to burst into a flaming torch in the weeks and months ahead.

For the first time in my life I met some Christians who actually believed and freely shared that Jesus Christ was a living reality in their lives. A subtle almost imperceptible breeze of fresh air began to cleanse away the dust and dry leaves that had accumulated on the floor of my being. As I look back now, I can see that the Lord Jesus had approached my tomb of Lazarus-like death and was beginning a new miracle of resurrection.

During the remaining weeks of the school year of 1970, as spring unfolded, unusual things began to happen. One of the students I was counseling came to my room one day to relate with great enthusiasm the experience he had had the night before at a little known prayer meeting held in a small town nearby. He evidently had encountered in a very real way the presence of the living God and was so deeply moved that he came seeking some explanation of what might have happened to him. I was totally unfamiliar with any so-called prayer meetings and was completely at a loss to explain what he had experienced. In fact, I was somewhat leery of it and tried to calm him down and reassure him that in a couple of days the excitement would subside and he would be back on an even keel.

The following week another student came with a similar story, bubbling with joy and excitement over meeting the Lord and hoping I could explain the meaning of it. I was still very much in the dark and felt quite inadequate to make any sense of it. One thing seemed certain, however: the experience of God was real for him. It occurred to me that if I was to be of any help counseling these students, I ought to find out about it.

The Lord used the next several weeks to sprinkle across my path many believers who eagerly witnessed to the power and loving presence of the Lord Jesus they had discovered through the Catholic pentecostal movement. Some were more direct than others, but often they would give me a book with that familiar comment: "Father, here's one you just have to read." I began to accumulate quite a collection of books from priests, sisters, and lay people which, of course, I didn't have a chance to read.

Early that summer I had to attend a convention in the South and had thrown the top book off of this stack into my suitcase with the hopes that I might have time to read it. It wasn't until I was on the plane coming home that I began to read *The Cross and the Switchblade*. Again, the mysterious hand of the Lord seemed evident for it turned out to be just the right book at the right time for me. It brought back a glimpse and almost a vicarious experience of what I had once dreamed priesthood might be like. The fires of hope began to burn with a new brightness as I began to sense how powerfully the Lord loved me and wanted to work in my life. It was the fastest plane ride I ever made. I couldn't wait to get to the next book on my stack, *Catholic Pentecostals* by Kevin Ranaghan. I began to pray between lines and an unquenchable thirst for the Lord started to invade my whole being. The more I read and prayed, the more I recognized the desert within and an overpowering desire for that fullness of life in Jesus that suddenly seemed so close and readily available. I made up my mind to go to one of those Thursday night prayer meetings to find out for myself if it could really be true.

All kinds of obstacles seemed to get in the way. Thursday after Thursday, schedule conflicts arose which kept me away. One Thursday in July some of my classmates called to go out to dinner. After a couple of drinks and a good dinner it was suddenly a quarter of eight and they each excused themselves to get back to the rectory for eight o'clock appointments. As I sat there alone wondering what to do, I remembered it was Thursday and the prayer meeting began at 8:00 p.m. Ah, this was my long awaited chance!

I slipped in the back door of the church basement and took a chair in the last circle, hoping I would go unnoticed without my collar on. There was a crowd of some three hundred people with their chairs arranged in concentric circles. As the prayer meeting progressed, I observed, in what seemed to be a very objective manner, that all those things I had read about in the books were happening. There was much joyful singing mingled with Scripture reading, praying in tongues, prophecy, teaching, and frequent spontaneous prayers of praise and thanksgiving.

When the meeting ended, I departed quickly, hoping no one had seen me. While driving back to the seminary, I began to wonder how come nothing happened to me like those unusual experiences others had related to me. It dawned on me that the best preparation for a prayer meeting probably wasn't to go out and have a couple of belts and a big meal.

That week I did a lot more reading about the charismatic renewal and quite a bit more praying which was starting to come easier now. A spirit of quiet anticipation began to arise and I couldn't wait for Thursday to come. Often in my reading I noticed references to prayer connected with fasting, something which was foreign to my experience. So as not to make the same mistake as the week before I decided to go all the way and try it. That Thursday I did fast and spent much of the day praying in preparation for the prayer meeting and the renewed life the Lord would bring me.

I was braver that night and, though I still didn't wear my clerics, I moved in from the fringe toward the middle of the circle of chairs. It was a totally different experience. Rather than being an onlooker and observer, I discovered to my joy that I was drawn very easily into the deep spirit of prayer and praise that filled the room. The hymns and Scripture readings and witnesses all seemed to be aimed directly at me. The time went so fast I hardly realized two hours had passed and the meeting was coming to an end. A new eagerness filled me when they announced, as they had the week before, that anyone who wanted special prayer would be welcome in a room upstairs where a team would pray with people.

This time instead of quickly slipping out the door I went directly upstairs to the prayer room. At that point the Lord did one of those quietly amazing things that formerly I would have called a coincidence, but have come to recognize as another sign of his living hand in all things. I ran into a Sister and friend who at one time had witnessed to me about the charismatic renewal. She must have seen the determined look on my face because she asked, "Where are you going?" I said, "I'm going up and get it!" She then inquired if I wanted anyone to pray with me and I assured her I did. She asked me to wait a minute, and gathered five people. Amazingly, all of them were friends of mine and at one time or another had spoken to me about the pentecostal movement and given me books to read. She didn't know them all and they didn't know each other. They didn't even come regularly to the prayer meetings, but all happened to be there that night.

They led me into a smaller room. We sat crosslegged in a

circle together on the floor and prayed. They explained briefly the baptism in the Holy Spirit which I was familiar with from my reading, and pointed out the promises of the Lord and his absolute faithfulness in carrying them out when we asked. They then encouraged me to renew my baptismal promises, to make a total commitment of my life to the Lord, and ask Jesus to baptize me in his Holy Spirit. I remember giving myself to the Lord in as full a way as I had ever done, for whatever he wanted, asking especially for the gift of preaching which had always been so difficult for me. They prayed with me through all of this. To this day, I'm amazed that I didn't feel some twinge of embarrassment that a Sister and five lay men and women were gently and easily leading me, a priest, into the Spirit. But it never crossed my mind.

It wasn't a long session. There were no fireworks or lightning bolts, but just the greatest peace and love and Godliness I'd ever experienced. In the following days and weeks a gradual, but quite remarkable transformation began to occur. A peace and joy surpassing all understanding filled me. I began to not only believe, but to actually know and experience the great love Jesus has for me. Prayer became the most enjoyable part of the day and seemed to permeate the whole day. It was becoming a lively, awesome, intimate exchange with the greatest friend I'd ever known. The real presence of the Lord was unmistakable. A fountain of living water sprang up within me bringing an overwhelming desire to praise him in everything. And miracle of miracles, instead of dreading the pulpit on Sundays, I actually couldn't wait to get up and preach the Good News. There was a new power in the Holy Spirit to proclaim the Lordship of Jesus Christ. Mass, confessions, counseling, teaching, all became golden opportunities to proclaim, introduce, and announce the risen Lord Jesus I had come to know in a personal way as my Lord and Savior. Somehow a corner was turned, a fire was ignited, a new life was begun that has made all the difference.

No longer is God's power a part of an unrealized vision of what I hoped for in a priest's life. The power of his Spirit working in me each day now brings new experiences of God's powerful mercy and love, healing, and salvation flowing out to his people. There is nothing more enjoyable in all the world than discovering that the Lord can use you. It's like putting your two drops worth in and seeing a flood take place as Jesus pours out in a new abundance his Holy Spirit to renew his people.

Praise the Lord Jesus Christ! Now and Forever!

Fr. John Comer / 2

Fr. John Comer was born in St. Louis, Missouri, March 6, 1938. He entered the seminary in high school at the Cardinal Glennon College. He was ordained a priest March 14, 1964, after finishing at the Kenrick Seminary.
He has since then worked as a high school teacher and as a parish priest in several different parishes. Currently, he is working with the Visitation Prayer Community in St. Louis.

Fr. John Comer

Friday the 13th is supposed to be an unlucky day. But I am thankful that God's ways are not ours, for on November 13, 1970, Jesus baptized me in the Holy Spirit. I had had for years what I considered a satisfactory relationship with God — I felt that I knew him deeply, and I occasionally experienced his closeness. But, thank God, *he* was not satisfied. He wanted to come even closer to me, to bring me into a personal relationship with the Trinity. Due to the change from Latin to English in the liturgy, I began to hear more and more about a person named Jesus Christ. The Holy Spirit gradually led me to an awareness that, while I knew God personally, I did not know this person Jesus Christ; rather, I knew *about* Jesus Christ. I couldn't witness to Jesus as one who had personally seen, heard, and known him; I found it much easier to call him Christ.

For two years, the Holy Spirit worked to give me a hunger to know Jesus. And I wasn't quietly cooperating, either; I was stubborn and proud, and tried to immerse myself in church activities. But finally, the Spirit got me to listen to my hunger, that hunger that is so necessary before one can share deeply in God's feast of love.

Finally, God led someone to invite me to the Visitation prayer meeting in St. Louis. That prayer meeting really bothered me, for my "I" had not yet given up. I thought, "These people are too happy and joyful; they must be sick, or some kind of fanatics. Why, they're actually praising Jesus as if they really knew him!" When someone would say, "Praise you, Jesus!" or "Praise you, Father!" I just wanted to run up the stairs and out of there. I would never have admitted it, but it scared me to death! The lack of true joy and peace and love in my own life made any expression of joy and peace and love look excessive.

But even in my resistance, the Lord was planting the seeds in me through his people. The Holy Spirit continued to work on me, and my hunger grew — above my fears, above my barriers, above all my intellectual abilities. God was destroying "the wisdom of the wise" in me so that I could accept the foolishness of his message. In the end, I let go and said an unconditional *yes* to Jesus. I asked him to be my Lord.

Being baptized in the Spirit was very quiet. I felt nothing happen, but another door had been opened in my life. Deep peace came into me, and I knew in my heart the personal presence of Jesus. As the Holy Spirit led me to my Saviour in repentance, I felt my sins and guilt lifted from me, and I knew that the way was open to the Father. The words came to me: "You shall know the truth, and the truth shall set you free; I am the Truth." What Jesus had accomplished on the cross had become real for me — the free gift of total forgiveness that I could never earn myself, but that I could receive from him.

As I submitted myself to Jesus as my Lord, my problems with submission to authority gradually disappeared. There was an increased awareness of myself as just one member of Jesus' body, the church, of the other members of his body, and of my responsibility to love and to share in the fellowship of Jesus' sufferings. Scripture opened up to me like a personal letter; prayer became a talking and listening relationship instead of a duty. It was a joy to see Jesus working in the sacrament of penance to not only forgive sins, but to heal the wounds they inflict. And no words can describe the change in my worship of God in the Mass, and the difference the Spirit made in the pulpit on Sunday morning! Before, I could never preach the word without writing each sermon out, and very seldom were my homilies about the "Good News." Now I discovered that the Spirit really leads and prepares and teaches us what to say to proclaim his message.

Soon I discovered the power of the Holy Spirit in another of my weaknesses — an area of sin. And since I knew my weakness, I could take no credit for my new strength in that area; I could only praise and thank the Lord. As I see more and more of his strength, I become more aware of my own weaknesses; yet at the same time I can better accept myself. For while I know that there are other areas of my life to be taken care of, I also know that Jesus is my Lord and that he is faithful. I know that he is praying for me and working for me all the time; that even when I fail to love, as I often do, he loves me and fits those failures into his plan.

Jesus loves me as I am, now! My Father loves me as his child, his son! It is great to be able to love myself and others in his love.

"Just as the Father has loved me, I have also loved you; abide in my love. If you keep my commandments, you will abide in my love; just as I have kept my Father's commandments and abide in his love. These things I have spoken to you, that my joy may be in you, and that your joy may be full. This is my commandment, that you love one another just as I have loved you. When the Helper comes, whom I will send to you from the Father, that is the Spirit of truth, who proceeds from the Father, he will bear witness of me, and you will bear witness also." (John 15:9-12, 26-27)

And the result is:

"By this we know that we abide in him and he in us, because he has given us of his Spirit. And we have beheld and bear witness that the Father has sent the Son to be the Savior of the world. And we have come to know, and have believed the love which God has for us." (1 John 4:13-14, 16)

Fr. Charles Antekeier / 3

Rev. Charles Antekeier was ordained in 1962, in Grand Rapids, Michigan. He has been actively involved in parish work and is now at St. Mary's parish in Grand Rapids.

Fr. Charles Antekeier

Just prior to my ordination in 1962, I recall "praying," telling God that he could send me any place in our diocese except Cheboygan. It was so far from my family and the friends with whom I had been in school for some twelve years. But God knows better than I what is best for me. When the assignments came out, Cheboygan was my destination. I loved the town. But despite that, a heavy burden was placed on my shoulders the first day there. Recognizing the importance of priestly fellowship, I told my pastor that I was going across the river to the other parish to meet the priest. He looked up from his desk with a remark that shocked me to my very depths: "We don't do that here!" It was not long before I found out that not only didn't the priests talk, but the whole city was divided by more than the river. One parish competed with the other in everything, parishioners, events, etc. I cried out, "My God, how can we spread your Kingdom? Your priests won't even speak to each other."

A year passed and somehow I persevered. A newly ordained priest was sent to a town just seventeen miles from me, and I thought that at last I would have someone to share with. Well, we did share — but we never shared God. He was a liberal from the word go and everything that was not meaningful to him did go. I was conservative — my work was to conserve everything. In 1962 I sometimes felt that I was doing all the Holy Spirit's work preserving doctrine in Northern Michigan — and believe me, it is not a nice role. It took me a long time to learn to let God do his work.

We both liked the outdoors, so we purchased beautiful Arabian horses and probed deep into the north woods. Each Monday, our day off, we would take our lunches and bathing suits and ride all day enjoying the quiet, the streams and hills, even running into unsuspecting deer. All this beauty, but we could never give thanks to God for sharing his beauty with man. We realized the folly in this. Two young men dedicated to bringing Jesus Christ to people and we could not share him with each other or even begin to share prayer. We tried reading current theology books during the week to discuss on Monday, but we were just incapable of carrying this out. Nothing worked.

One day on the way to a meeting in the midst of a snow storm, we began to spin on the ice. Immediately I began praying out loud. We did not hit another car, a telephone pole or a reflector on the side of the road — we did end up in a snow bank. My friend simply put the car in reverse and got back on the road. I sighed, "Thanks be to God," but he responded, "What good is prayer going to do? If you are going to get in an accident, you are going to get in an accident. What good is prayer going to do?"

Shortly after this I received a transfer to a parish in Grand Rapids. I had been gone a year from the north and had not seen my friend during that time. In September of 1967 I was scheduled for a retreat at St. Lazare and again met my friend, but this time he was a changed person. After the first conference he told me that he was praying for me. I told him that I didn't need that kind of prayer;

remember, *he* was the one who did not believe in prayer. After that conference I felt moved to look him up, but I fought the idea. "God," I prayed, "I want to talk to and about you on this retreat, not about horses." The Lord persisted and I gave in, found out his room number, and knocked on his door. "Do you want to talk?" I asked. "Do I!" was his reply.

This was the story he had to tell me. The person I thought was a cocky young priest was a man going through hell trying to find some meaning in his priesthood. The person I thought was a dynamic speaker, with a keen mind and a feeling for young people, was a priest frustrated because he did not know the power of God's word which he daily ministered. He could not help one of all the teenagers who came to him for help by bringing them to the real truth. He hungered for God's help. One day he opened the *National Catholic Reporter* and was struck by this headline: "Students Gather Enjoying Praying." Enjoying prayer? He did not know how to pray, much less enjoy it. The article described the charismatic happenings at Notre Dame. At the first opportunity he traveled to South Bend to investigate. He liked what he saw — large groups of students and faculty meeting for hours in deep prayer. He returned up north and read everything he could get his hands on that referred to the Holy Spirit. And then he was led to read the Bible.

At this time he felt that he should travel to Grand Rapids to meet and open his heart to a humble man of God, of the Assembly of God church. In those days we did little talking with folks of other faiths and almost no praying, especially with the Assembly of God people. My friend gave in to the Lord and started his trip to Grand Rapids. Halfway down he decided this was foolish. "What if the bishop hears of this?" he thought. His parents lived in Grand Rapids so he continued on the trip with the idea of visiting them. As he was driving into the city he was thinking, "I wonder if I could have found that pastor's church had I been looking for it?" He drove around; sure enough he found it. He continued to muse, "I wonder if I were interested, if I could find the pastor." He got out of his car and walked up to a man cutting the lawn in front of the church. "I don't imagine Pastor Hogan is around," my friend blurted out. "I am Pastor Hogan," the man with the lawn mower answered. He brought him into his office and there, after listening to my friend open his heart, he said simply, "You are a proud young priest who is trying to do all the work yourself. Let the Spirit of God work through you." My friend knelt and the pastor laid hands on him in prayer. Tears of joy gushed from his eyes and he knew that his life was changed. The young man who did not believe in prayer was changed into a man of deep prayer. As my friend shared this with me — we who could never share God spent three hours together praising God for his goodness — I received the baptism of the Holy Spirit.

I can recall the exact location where we walked. It was as though the skies opened and I saw Jesus coming in great power. The words I heard myself say were: "He's coming, Jesus Christ is coming — He's here and knows us. He is in the Church and cares. Praise God!" This was the first time I had said "Praise God," but I was soon to find out that there were going to be many firsts in my life for I too had been changed. The heavy burden I felt because of Christian separation and division was lifted from me. I knew that God was in the Church and had never deserted us. A deep joy came over me, a love for Scripture developed, and I could see people with new eyes as children of a loving

Father in heaven. My preaching changed critically. I remember one Sunday many years ago when I prayed before getting in the pulpit, "Let me, Lord, preach you — not myself — and as a sign that you were preached, don't let one person after Mass say it was a good sermon." That sermon was different. I experienced the words going out and entering the hearts of everyone present and, what was even more wonderful, I was not building myself up as a great preacher. But after Mass not one person came up to say it was a good sermon. I knew it was a good sermon — the Spirit of God had given it — but as I walked back into the sanctuary I said, "God, don't take me so seriously." I had come that close to letting God work through me, but I didn't like the idea of his getting all the credit. It wasn't until September 1967, four years later, that Jesus again began to preach his sermons through me, as I experienced the baptism of the Holy Spirit.

Fr. Matt Killian / 4

Rev. Matthew Killian, O.C.S.O., is a monk of Holy Cross Abbey, Berryville, Virginia. He has an M.A. in theology, and has served as prior and as master of novices in his monastery. Fr. Killian also spent several years in France in a hermitage.

Fr. Matt Killian

My first gropings for the baptism in the Holy Spirit came in Rome. I was sent there by my monastery to study for a master's degree in theology. In the winter of 1961, I fell ill with pneumonia and spent six weeks in the infirmary. While there I was visited almost daily by a French monk who was very interested in the eremetical life.

My acceptance of the Saviour had occurred almost twenty years ago, just prior to my entrance into the monastery. It was the result of the discovery of prayer. Prayer became so important to me that I decided to devote my entire life to it. In the Roman infirmary, the hermit's life seemed a wonderful way to crown a vocation to prayer. It was a challenge to live with and for God alone; not oblivious of other men, but hoping to help them in their life search through the exclusiveness of and fidelity to my own search.

After we received our degrees, my French friend and I parted, each to his own monastery, but not before agreeing that we both should make practical efforts toward the realization of our desires.

I was quickly disappointed when, upon arriving home, I was appointed prior of the monastery and, later, master of novices. That seemed to ice any possibilities I might have had of fulfilling my hope. But in the late summer of 1965, I heard my friend had found an excellent site for a hermitage in the Vosges mountains in northeastern France. He desired that I come and enter with him upon this life as soon as possible. I referred the request to my superiors, and was quite surprised when they gave me the go ahead sign.

We began our hermit's life on November 9, 1965. The setting was beautiful but very austere: an old stone house lacking electricity, running water, toilet facilities, and using wood for fuel. It was just off the crest of a mountain in a fir forest, miles from the nearest town. The following year, 1966, was to prove the most difficult year of my life. At first it was the physical rigors of the situation: the cold and the snow went on for months, and then I was unused to such poverty, darkness, and diet. We soon learned that the house was infested with rats. Around Easter time our only food was potatoes. The summer brought some respite from these difficulties, but my companion and I then began to experience difficulty in getting along with each other. It was a bitter pill to swallow: that in our search for a life of deeper union with God, we had such a problem in living with one another.

Lent and Easter time had enkindled an ardent desire in me for God's grace. I could not articulate then what I was looking for, except for the fact that the feast of Pentecost was its focus. However, that year the feast passed by with little alleviation of my spiritual hunger. Although the following year was easier physically, the same aching hunger and expectation persisted throughout the Paschal cycle. By then solitude was weighing heavily upon me. A foreshadowing of what was in store for me came a few days after Pentecost, when I was visited by the abbot of our monastery and he remarked how happy he would be if I could return.

Return seemed to be a spiritual step backward: having put my hand to the plow, I thought I should keep on going. But in the succeeding months other signs appeared indicating God's will. In the fall of 1967, my companion had to leave the hermitage and it was put up for sale. I had no funds to build another in France, so I thought more and more of returning. The state of turmoil in our own country at that time also attracted me, for I felt that I should share its difficulties in a more immediate way, even though prayer was my only way of helping out.

As the third Paschal cycle began, I knew that this time I would find fulfillment. I left the mountain hermitage on Easter Sunday and was soon back in my Virginia monastery. About a week before Ascension Thursday I was called to the visiting parlor to speak to two housewives who had come to inquire about the life of prayer. At the end of an hour of conversation, I was asked if I knew anything about the Pentecostal movement. When I professed my ignorance, they asked me to read some articles which they left with me. A few days later I received a letter from each woman. And then on the Monday following, since I wanted to answer their letters, I decided to read the articles. I was carrying them down to the scriptorium when one of the novices who had not spoken to me, as yet, since my return, accosted me. Abruptly he asked if I knew anything of the Pentecostal movement. Again a negative reply. But now my interest was up. I showed him the articles in my hand. He told me he and another novice were going to prepare for the feast of Pentecost by praying together, seeking this baptism in the Holy Spirit. I asked him if I could join them; and we began on the feast of the Ascension. We prayed daily for about an hour, sometimes praying over one another. Other monks joined us until we were about ten. On the vigil we prayed all night through, surprised how quickly the time went by. I foolishly expected, I guess, to be engulfed in tongues of fire at the concelebrated mass on the morrow, and, of course, was disappointed when nothing like that happened. However at vesper-time I was told a Pentecostal minister was coming the following day to pray with us. Certainty of fulfillment immediately filled my heart. I did not realize then that Pentecost Monday was the fifth anniversary of Pope John's death.

Reverend Bob Topping of the Church at Northern Virginia came and prayed with us for the Baptism. As he prayed over me I felt nothing though he said I could pray in tongues before I went downstairs. My disposition was a tremendous desire for the fulfillment in me of the Father's promise: the coming of the Spirit of God in fullness. Almost all of us were prayed over. Later that afternoon one of the brethren began to pray in tongues. On the following day at our prayer meeting, he said he would pray in tongues before us for our edification and encouragement. As he did so, I began to feel a warmth in my lower legs that started to climb my body. It passed my waist, then chest, but stopped at my neck. I felt if it had continued I, too, would be speaking in tongues. But there was some inhibition that was preventing it from surfacing. Perhaps it was the presence of others, I thought. So later that afternoon, while alone in the back of the church, I petitioned God to give me this grace and ventured forth by faith into this new language. Since that time, almost daily I have prayed or sung in tongues.

Before I close this testimony of God's goodness, I would like to mention a reflection that often has come to me. Although two weeks previous to my baptism in the Holy

Spirit I hardly knew of its existence, the experience of tongues was not something that dropped out of the blue and was wholly unrelated to my life. It was truly a culminating experience for me of the Paschal mystery that had been going on for three years. Like deliverance to the psalmist or the tongues of fire to the apostles, it began a new dimension in my life. By it I have entered into a life of more constant prayer; not so dependent upon solitude and ascetical effort. The housewives and novices taught me this lesson. Nor is it bound up so exclusively in prayer-formulas and time spent in church. There is greater freedom in that regard. But the one radicalized demand is faith: faith in God working in the *Now*. He has done much in the past for us, and will do much in the future, but it is, above all, at this *present* moment that the blessed Spirit of God is present and active.

One last thought: many Protestant charismatics have told me that they expect great things of the Pentecostal movement in the Catholic Church. My own experience makes me agree. Our church is now passing through the dark night of the passion; it, like Jesus on the cross, feels the abandonment of the Father. Its confusion, darkness and suffering reminds me of that year 1966. I know patience, prayer and faith in the Father's promise will bring to it the full experience of Pentecost. God shares with all who believe the victory of Christ's resurrection; and this is the victory that overcomes the world: our faith. I sense, also, that the world, and especially our own country, even waits, expects and wants to be thus overcome.

Fr. William O'Brien / 5

Rev. William O'Brien is a diocesan priest in the Archdiocese of Newark, New Jersey; after ordination, he spent seven years in parish work and is now the university chaplain at Fairleigh Dickinson University, Rutherford, N.J. He is also one of the leaders in the Ignatius House Community in Rutherford.

Fr. William O'Brien

It is winter now, the hills of northern Virginia are cold and covered with frost. The meadows are drained of their color and the trees leave only austere marks against the sky. The monastery is peaceful and silent. The monks of Holy Cross Abbey have offered me the hospitality of their Trappist life for a month. It has been a great gift to live here in an atmosphere of prayer where God is sought all the time. That I am doing this and not vacationing under a palm tree somewhere is all part of the story I would like to share with you.

I am a diocesan priest from the Archdiocese of Newark, New Jersey. My life as a priest spans twelve years. The first seven of those years were spent as a curate in Our Lady of Victories parish, Jersey City, the last five years as a university chaplain at Fairleigh Dickinson University, Rutherford, N.J. I don't have a long list of academic accomplishments nor a career of distinguished sanctity in the service of the Lord. I am just one of the many ordinary men who serve the Church as its priests. I am a product of the system: Catholic grammar school, Jesuit prep school, seminary. By today's standards, I suppose I ought to feel brainwashed or badly cheated but I don't. I have many reservations and criticisms of the way I was educated and trained in Catholicism; however, at thirty-seven I am not bitter, only a little sad that so many mistakes were made.

When I started out as a university chaplain my ideas were a little different. Seven years of parochial work had left me with a general sense of frustration. What I saw as the ordinary functioning of priestly ministry seemed to have little or no impact on people's individual lives nor on the urban environment. I administered sacraments by the hundreds and preached every Sunday. Nothing changed; our love for God and for one another didn't seem to move very much. The organizational form of the parish as well as the ministry I exercized didn't seem to have much power. When I observed the larger body of the Church, I thought the hierarchy had failed to give the kind of leadership that was needed. I listened to other priests as they lost hope that the Church could possibly be renewed to meet the needs of our times.

I don't think my attitudes are unfamiliar; they typify most priests my age. I have come to question many things about the Church and its functioning because I want her to be the vehicle of God's saving love for the world. The Church, although I love her dearly, is a bit tarnished by sin, not only in its individual members but in its structure. The Bride of Christ is a paradox. On the one hand seemingly too sinful to have anything divine about it, and on the other, possessing the sublime spirituality of being the body of the living, risen Jesus.

The criticisms and cynicism of our fellow priests as well as our reading fare can have a very negative effect on us. Our friends will either influence us to see nothing of value in the Church and its life or they will build up our faith. These are confusing times and, for all that, there is probably no area of ministry within the Catholic Church that has felt the effect of the current confusion as much as the campus ministry.

When I left the parochial ministry to go to the University campus, I had great hope for the retreats, discussions, movies, liturgies, and social action programs that I would be able to offer to a hungry student body. It took me about six months to discover that the students weren't hungry and my great programs produced nothing. When I went to professional campus ministry meetings, my colleagues seemed just as unsuccessful. The good news at these meetings was the Secular City, involvement in the Revolution, and general uncertainty about what a campus minister was supposed to be. A great sense of confusion and doubt began to overtake me.

When I left the parish for the campus, I also left behind me rectory living. I was furnished with an apartment near the campus that I shared with another priest. We had no community life together, in fact, we only shared a few meals together in the course of the year we shared the apartment. At the end of that year my companion left the active ministry. I felt rather isolated; there wasn't any kind of spiritual community to support me or help me. Most of my daily contacts were with non-believers. There didn't seem to be very many people in my new world who believed or even seemed to care about Jesus Christ. Most of the students I talked to would easily recite their objections to me. There was a very challenging pluralism in the secular university and at first it appeared overwhelming.

My experience at apartment living revealed many things to me about myself. At thirty-two I was for the first time totally responsible for my life. There was no structure, no set of norms to go by. What would happen depended a great deal on my initiative. Rectory life had provided many safeguards and offered a good deal of freedom from things like cleaning house, shopping for food, and paying the telephone bill. I began to realize that all of this had not helped me to grow, in actuality I had little or no sense of responsibility for the way the rectory was maintained.

My life was not only in a phase of physical and emotional development, spiritually I became disorganized. I have always tried to maintain a daily time for prayer, but now my schedule had to adapt to the times when students wanted to talk, and that seemed to be mostly at night. Needless to say the mornings weren't too good after being up to one or two a.m. conversing with someone. The sum total of six months as a campus minister was doubt about the relevancy of the Gospel, about the priesthood, and about what I could do for the students I wanted to help.

I had been actively involved with the Cursillo Movement for several years. Making the Cursillo had been a significant spiritual step in my life. I had continued my interest in the movement and had met many alive Christians through it. A weekend workshop for all of the priests and lay leaders in the diocese was planned for February, 1969. I decided I would go, since I felt in need of some spiritual nourishment.

The workshop was conducted by a team of lay people and a priest. Steve Clark of Ann Arbor, Bob Morris of Cleveland, Bill Luff from Reno, and Fr. John Randall of Providence were members of the team. As I sat through the talks and discussions, I was overwhelmed by the faith to which they gave witness. As I listened, I began to realize they had something I didn't have; their faith was alive. They spoke about prayer as access to the living Jesus and the power of the Holy Spirit. As I listened I realized that my faith was at a pretty low ebb. Whatever it was these people had, I needed and wanted. I never thought of asking them at the time. I had never heard of the baptism of the Holy Spirit or the charismatic renewal. All I knew was that faith was a gift from the Lord and if I prayed he could give it to me. I did not understand what had happened to me that weekend, but I left with a new dimension of faith that I didn't have before.

The next morning I was scheduled to offer Mass in one of the local parish churches. I arrived early so that I could begin the day with prayer. At the conclusion of the prayer time, I asked the Lord to lead me in my work with the students that day, to lead me to the person who was searching for him.

As the morning went by the prayer drifted to the back of my mind. By lunch time I had pretty much forgotten it. When I went to the cafeteria to eat, I sat at table with a group of laughing chatting students. In the midst of the joking one of the young men unexpectedly asked, "Father, what does God really mean to you?" My answer took just a few minutes. Then I got up to leave. The student followed me and said, "Father, you believe so much what you said that I just want to talk to you for awhile." The incident made me aware of the prayer I had made that morning. The Lord was at work. He had given me a faith in him alive enough for someone to notice and he was pointing my attention to someone who was sincerely searching for him. This was the first of a number of similar incidents that awakened me to a whole new world of the Holy Spirit's activity in my life and ministry.

Following the Cursillo workshop, a few priests began to meet each week to pray. It was a great help to be able to share my experiences with a few brothers and to be built up by listening to them. Shared prayer was a new experience in my life. It made me hungry to spend more time alone with the Lord. The Scriptures, too, were alive and began to mean a great deal to me. I began to approach them for the first time as God's word spoken directly to me. I began to listen to what the Lord was trying to say to me through the Psalms of the Office and the reading of Scripture that I did every day.

My work among the students still wasn't progressing very much. I wanted to share with them what was happening to me but I didn't know how. Finally I decided simply to ask them to come together to pray, trusting that the Lord could do for them what he did for me. At that time the student organization was made up of about ten students. Our first attempt at shared prayer was rather difficult. No one was interested except two girls. Our shared prayer sessions dwindled to them and myself after the first few times. God really blessed our feeble attempts at trying to reach him. The Holy Spirit began to work in the hearts of the two young women.

One day, about halfway through the spring semester of 1969, I received a phone call from a priest friend of mine, telling me that he had met two young men who were interested in becoming lay volunteers in the campus ministry. I was excited by the possibility, maybe the Lord was at work again. One of the young men was available that day to come over to talk to me. That afternoon Les Williams, then a junior at Fordham University, came to see me. After we had talked for awhile, he asked me to pray with him. I was amazed at such a request coming from a young man — I wasn't used to college students who wanted to pray. While we were praying, I took the New Testament and opened it. I don't remember the exact text my eyes fell upon, I only remember that I was struck by the words,

"This man has been sent by God." Time has proved that message to have been true. Les had been involved in the charismatic group at Fordham and it was through him and a few others that I came to know about the baptism of the Holy Spirit and the charismatic renewal.

At first, I was very hesitant about all the terminology. It sounded too Protestant to me. I hadn't read anything from Catholic sources about it and I was concerned that it might all be unorthodox or a complete delusion. A few weeks later I was reading a copy of *America* and noticed a little blurb about a conference on the charismatic renewal to be held at Notre Dame at the beginning of June. I decided to go and find out for myself what all this was about. At this point I had never been to a charismatic prayer meeting.

In June I traveled to Notre Dame and arrived on a Friday evening. I had difficulty finding the meeting; not too many people had heard of it. I finally found a prayer meeting in progress in the Field House. When I walked into the gym about 400 or 500 people were gathered in a circle praying. I was only there a few minutes and they began praying and singing in tongues. It was the first time I had ever heard the strange sound and melodies. I listened, and since it wasn't at all a frenzy, I decided to wait and see what else happened before I rendered my judgement. The prayer meeting was very peaceful and orderly but what impressed me most was the witnessing and spontaneous prayers. I noticed immediately one distinctive quality about the prayer. It was prayer centered on God, not on self. It wasn't just "Lord, do this for me or make me into that," but a prayer of adoration and worship of God for himself. By the end of the meeting I was convinced that the Holy Spirit was indeed manifesting himself in these people.

The next day workshops were offered on different subjects, among them the baptism of the Holy Spirit. Kevin Ranaghan gave an excellent presentation describing the experience of the baptism of the Spirit. The qualities of this enlivening of the Spirit were the same as I had experienced after attending the Cursillo workshop a few months before. I did experience a deepening of faith, a coming alive to the word of God, a sense of the leading of the Holy Spirit. I had not experienced praying in tongues or any other charismatic gift. I wanted to be sure that I wasn't kidding myself so I asked the helpers at the workshops to pray with me to receive the baptism of the Holy Spirit. I did not experience anything at the time they prayed for me, but I felt peaceful about the whole thing.

A few weeks later I was praying with a few brother priests who had been baptized in the Spirit. They began praying in tongues; as they did I effortlessly and without even thinking about it just joined in. I have, since then, experienced the gifts of prophecy, healing and discernment.

At this point you may very well ask whether I know these things are from God or have been led astray by some kind of self delusion. All that I can answer is that certain objective things have happened that are not my imagination. I have witnessed the fruits of the Holy Spirit that Saint Paul mentions being manifested along with these gifts. In my own life it has brought about at least the desire for a deep conversion of life.

The greatest real sign I have had and continue to have is what has happened in my ministry. In September, 1969, four people gathered to pray on Thursday evenings. Now, in January, 1973, between 175 and 200 people gather to pray on Thursday evenings.

I have witnessed a return of these young people to the sacramental life of the Church and to attending Mass. I have witnessed people's lives being changed and staying changed. If these aren't the signs of God's work, what is?

In the summer of 1970 about a dozen young men came to live at the Newman Center for a summer of community living. It was to be an experiment in Christian community. The summer was so successful that a similar project was planned for the following year. During the winter four of the young men decided to come and stay at the Newman Center for the 1970-71 school year and work on the campus and among the people who were coming to the prayer meeting.

Through our sharing and praying we began to look rather seriously at what God was asking us to do in living in a community together. We saw that we needed a deepening of our own spiritual lives as well as the bond that would hold us together.

With the help of a Jesuit friend, we were able to make the thirty-day Spiritual Exercises of St. Ignatius at St. Andrew's Hall, Syracuse, New York. It was a great experience for all of us, and has had a profound effect on us ever since.

Our community now numbers about seventy people who have committed themselves. About forty of these people are living in small groups in and around the University. These people have agreed to a certain life-style of Christianity in community. That means morning and evening prayer together, sharing a meal once a day and trying to live as brothers and sisters in the Lord.

What has happened to me personally and in the community that has gathered in Rutherford is, I believe, the work of the Holy Spirit. The charismatic renewal may not answer every theological question or be the panacea for all the problems of the Church, but it does offer us access to power, power that can change men's hearts and even our own. I feel more alive now than when I was ordained. Instead of being bankrupt and powerless in the face of an unbelieving world, I can now rely on the power of the Holy Spirit to bring the inner change that my rather uneloquent words or fancy footwork could never do.

Fr. Luke Rigby / 6

Rev. Luke Rigby, O.S.B., was ordained in the Benedictine order in 1950. After several years of high school teaching and parish work in his native England, he came to the United States in 1955 as a treasurer of a new Benedictine foundation in St. Louis, Missouri, St. Louis Priory. He was appointed prior in 1967, an appointment which was reconfirmed by election when St. Louis became an independent priory in July, 1973.

Fr. Luke Rigby

The very fact that I was at the Fifth International Conference on the Catholic Charismatic Renewal seemed a little strange. Some of the nearby Sisters of the Visitation were interested and they sent me the brochure, with a fairly strong suggestion that I come. The application said that registration would be limited to 2500 people, so I was secretly hoping and praying to be turned down. But it did not happen that way, and there were those who needed space in the car I would be driving. So on a hot, sticky Friday afternoon in June, we arrived at Notre Dame.

The opening session started at 8 p.m. in the Stepan Center — an un-air-conditioned geodesic dome jammed with small wooden folding chairs. Despite the announced limit, there were around 5000 people crowded in the Center. I don't like large crowds, and what an assortment of people! Giggling high school kids, barefoot hippies, sisters of every age and habit, priests, and a great number of people of all ages. I wasn't at all comfortable with the very evident cheerfulness and togetherness, and all the hugging and kissing that accompanied it. I found it remarkable that such a motley crowd had enough in common to be there together, but I did not feel a part of them.

Then the meeting began, and it was immediately evident what these people had in common. A small guitar group started things off. Five thousand people singing, "All of my life, I will sing praise to my God..." had to be impressive. There was no rush through a brief introductory prayer to get started with business; there were twenty minutes of prayer — vocal prayer, silent prayer, and prayer in tongues, rising and falling in song to die away together. I was impressed, but distracted by the unaccustomed gestures — the muttered prayers and raised hands — and my own clamoring questions. The talks that followed were balanced and restrained; I could see that this was not merely a group of unsure people looking desperately for answers they had not been able to find in the church of the past.

But by lunch time the next day I was feeling even more discontented and apart from all the crowd milling around me. I can only put down my extreme awareness of how it was all affecting me to the weight of the life-style that was evident all around me; or perhaps it was my fear and prejudice that heightened my awareness of this life-style and made me so judgmental. I recall feeling quite clearly that I had made the effort to go to Notre Dame, had left myself open to whatever call God might be making to me concerning the charismatic renewal, and it finally seemed clear to me that this was not for me, that I did not need to involve myself in this form of approach to God, and so on. I wanted to further test this feeling in prayer, so one of my Benedictine brethren, Fr. Ian Petit, and I prayed that God would make it clear once and for all what he wanted of me in relation to the charismatic renewal. A few minutes later, Fr. Ian ran into Fr. George Kosicki.

Somehow, Fr. George was able to get free from his work in the conference long enough to meet with me later in the afternoon. I explained how I was at once attracted to and uncertain of the charismatic movement. I had had previous contacts with people involved in the movement who had impressed me with their prayerfulness and openness, but I never felt at ease with their style of prayer and enthusiastic display of affection. I did not find the prayer meetings near my home in St. Louis congenial, and I found the impact of the conference a little more than I could take.

I also told George that I felt I had been baptized in the Spirit some time back in my monastic life, although it wasn't a specific experience that I could pinpoint. (I don't think I told him that I was also frightened of the whole idea.) But I asked him to pray with me that I might do whatever the Spirit wanted and that I might follow where he was leading me.

George replied that all my concern with the baptism of the Spirit didn't worry him; I had lived in the Spirit as a priest and a monk. But he said that we all have a tendency to restrict the Holy Spirit's work within us, so he suggested that we pray for a continued and constant deepening of the influence and power of the Spirit. We began to pray together, sitting right in main quadrangle of the campus, with groups of people walking and chatting and praying all around us. A sister whom I knew came up with another priest to join in the prayer over me, and then two or three more people, complete strangers, joined us. There I was, sitting on the bench in the middle of the quadrangle with people at my feet, standing behind me, sitting on either side of me, and all of them praying over me. They prayed in silence and aloud; they prayed in tongues and sang in tongues; they sang a couple of short hymns. They prayed that the Lord would come to me in a special way in the Spirit, in the way that he had come to each of them.

During the course of this prayer, I asked the Lord to

give a sign that this was what he wanted for me. Such a prayer was, and still is, foreign to me, but this was an unusual situation. I asked that two sisters from the Visitation community, who had been praying for me for a long time, could come by to share this with me. Nothing happened. I prayed again, asking the Lord for a greater faith, for the faith of the Gospels, and looked up to see them walking on the grass a hundred feet away. As they ran up to join our little group, I heard one of them say, "If we're praying for you, it must be a miracle!"

When George brought the prayer to a close, my first thought was to get away where I could be alone with the Lord and try to sort everything out. But I couldn't find any place to be alone, and I think this was for the best. For the most remarkable effect of this prayer was that I suddenly realized I was one with the rest of the crowd. All that had grated on me paled into insignificance, and all that was good — the prayerfulness, the joy, the dedication, the concern for one another — became much more evident.

When I returned to St. Louis from the conference, I reflected upon many great blessings from this occasion. One of the immediate results was a much greater awareness of the battle between light and darkness, between the powers of God and the powers of evil. I think that before, I had let my awareness of this truth of Christian life slip away. I too easily thought of problems and complications as almost a personal affront, I wished the church and the monastery to be a refuge from the battles of life. But now I can see my place in the battle more clearly; I can identify my problems and sufferings with the Lord and share in his life and work. I can see my life more readily and easily in the light of the teaching of Jesus.

I have found that my Scripture reading and prayer are deeper and more alive; I've experienced a praise and worship of God that goes beyond my previous experience. In the Divine Office and in my mental prayer I return to an aliveness, I grasp for the gift that has been given me and respond to it more often and easily. I appreciate more and more the importance of shared prayer, both in the nearby prayer group and in a small group here in our monastic community.

It is so clear to me that I have been given a new gift. I remember the words of our Lord about taking out of the treasure house things new and old. It's easy to forget that life is a continual renewal, to become stale and stop looking for the things which are newly offered. The Lord had given me faith in him long ago, but now he has given me a new gift to bring that faith to life; he is showing me through the whole of my being that I must believe in him and trust him, that all my efforts and work and decisions must be based in him and founded in his Word. This charismatic renewal is not inviting us to retreat from our day-to-day problems into a spiritual world, but rather to place the root, foundation, and base of our lives in the Lord.

For all he has done for me, I praise the Lord.

Fr. Michael Scanlan / 7

Rev. Michael Scanlan, a Franciscan of the Third Order
Regular, was born in Far Rockaway, New York, in 1931.
He has a B.A. from Williams College, a J.D. from Harvard,
and has done graduate studies in political science and
higher education at the Catholic University of America.
Since his ordination in 1964, he has been lecturer in
theology and dean of Steubenville College, Ohio, and is
presently rector president of St. Francis Seminary in
Loretto, Pennsylvania.
A member of the New York Bar Association, Fr. Scanlan
is a former U.S.A.F. Staff Judge Advocate, and has held
positions in a wide variety of professional organizations.
His articles have appeared in a number of religious perio-
dicals, and he has published a book, *Power in Penance.*

Fr. Michael Scanlan

My life changed drastically during 1969. For five years, I had been dean of the college at Steubenville, Ohio. I was happy with my job and I took satisfaction in doing the dean's work as efficiently as I was able. Outside the college, I was deeply involved in Cursillos. I also worked very closely with some black power groups in the inner city, I was involved in some ecumenical programs, and I was even first president of the Citizens for Clean Air in Steubenville. I was beginning to feel satisfied with my projects and I began to think I might be in Steubenville for the rest of my life.

Then I was unexpectedly elected to our provincial Curia, the five-man body that makes major policy for the Franciscan province. Soon after that, I was elected rector president of St. Francis Seminary in Loretto and superior of our community there. St. Francis is a major seminary serving seminarians from fifteen dioceses as well as our own Franciscan seminarians, and it dawned on me that I had been given an overwhelming responsibility. Before, I could be an efficient dean and do my meaningful work in the community. Now I had to be someone reflecting Christ. I had to be the kind of person who could show others what a priest could be. I had to be an encouragement for seminarians to persevere to the priesthood and for my fellow priests in our community to be better priests. This burden weighed very heavily on my shoulders. It frightened me.

I had always tried for the top success position. Inevitably I fell short of the top but achieved enough success to start a new climb on another staircase. When I was studying at Harvard Law, I tried so hard to be the best student that they finally had to admit me to the infirmary for some rest. Later I became a Judge Advocate in the Air Force and immediately tried to solve all the military justice problems in the eastern United States. Again I collapsed from exhaustion. I did the same thing in some of my inner city work, letting the problems and the work load build to the point of collapse.

This time I knew I couldn't wait until the work dominated me. I told the Lord that this was the end of my self-made programs and did my best to ask him to take over.

I hadn't read anything about Catholic pentecostals except some sensational headlines and stories about kooky things going on at Notre Dame, and I was not inclined to pursue it. Yet when a very close friend of mine, the superior of a women's Carmelite monastery nearby, told me about being baptized in the Holy Spirit, I don't remember even questioning what she said. We sat in the visiting room of the monastery and she just told me very simply what had happened to her since being prayed with. I thought to myself: "Yes, yes, this has to be for me. If being baptized in the Spirit can make such fantastic changes in her after twenty-three years of contemplative life, then it's definitely something I need right now."

I had to wait about five weeks. I read a little, but mostly just grew in hunger of the Spirit. Then, Fr. Jim Ferry from New Jersey came to St. Francis College to give a talk on pentecostalism. Every time he mentioned the name "Jesus" I felt as if someone was setting off sparks in me. The desire for Jesus was so strong I thought it would break through my chest. Later, Fr. Jim asked if anyone wanted to pray for anything. Before I knew it, I was kneeling in the middle of a group of about thirty people asking to be baptized in the Holy Spirit. They laid hands on me and immediately I received a tremendous peace right down to the balls of my feet. It completely filled me with a new sense of being, deep within me. It was glorious. I later joined a group praying over a priest for an increase in wisdom. But every time I tried to pray over this man in English, it came out in another tongue. That night, I woke up about twelve times to find myself praying. It was prayer I had never known before, a beautiful sense of the Holy Spirit crying out inside me. I knew that Jesus as Risen Lord had entered my life.

My work as a priest changed dramatically. My preaching became a proclamation of the Good News of Christ. My counseling included more prayer for healing. My confessional work involved revelatory gifts such as knowing what a person's problem was before he said it, or seeing a completely different approach to a problem than the one the person had. Prayer itself eventually took on a more contemplative orientation. I violated the rules I set for myself as a busy college administrator and gave the time between 8 and 10 every morning to the Lord, and found that I accomplished more between 10 and 12 than I used to between 8 and 12.

One of the biggest changes I experienced was a new courage and strength to state what I knew was right, even though my statements might be uncomfortable and unpopular. This happened most dramatically in connection with the conspiracy trial of Fr. Philip Berrigan and the others in Harrisburg. I had been a criminal lawyer; I had worked in a district attorney's office, in a public defender's office, and in the Judge Advocate's corps of the Air Force. I spoke publicly against the unjust practices the government employed in prosecuting the case. I did not totally agree with the Berrigan group's manner of protest; it contained some elements that seemed inconsistent with gospel peace. But the defendants certainly deserved justice. I was amazed that my activities in their behalf were marked by a new serenity and that people were moved to gospel commitments.

I shall end by sharing something which may enable other priests to relate their experiences to this new charismatic life. Seven years ago, I was in a little Piper Cub flying across Ohio from a meeting, when we hit a vicious hailstorm. The wings started to flap, the plane started to buckle, we dropped in air pockets, and we started to spin around. I became absolutely convinced that I would be dead in five minutes. When I turned to the Lord he gave me a deep sense of peace. I had never felt so utterly and completely secure in my whole life. I tasted his glory, majesty and beauty so profoundly that I became indifferent to whether or not the plane crashed. The pilot did put the plane into a nose dive, caught a current of air at the bottom of the storm, and landed.

The experience that the Lord gave me of himself for a moment in that airplane is the same as the one he has been giving me frequently since being baptized in the Spirit. He is the Lord — and that's all that counts.

Fr. Charles Magsam / 8

Rev. Charles Magsam, M.M., was ordained in 1933. After ordination, he spent several years in Rome for further studies. He taught in the novitiate for many years and also spent time giving retreats in Africa and the Orient. At present, he is working in Chile as a missionary. He has published two books in English, *The Inner Life of Worship* and *Theology and Practice of Love,* and two in Spanish, *Orientacion Personal* and *Renovacion Charismatica.*

Fr. Charles Magsam

After eight years of missionary work in Chile, the last two in Talcahuano with special emphasis on Bible-study groups, I was put on loan to do two writing projects in the States. At the time of my return to the States I felt pulled apart, so drained and exhausted by missionary work that it was difficult to concentrate or even pray. My efforts to organize the first project were a continuous frustration.

Within the first few weeks of my arrival, I began attending weekly charismatic Bible-prayer meetings. In the first meeting I was too paralyzed by fears to even open my mouth, but slowly and with great effort I began to participate actively. Soon I was participating in several meetings a week with different groups. We also formed a Bible-prayer group of priests where I got to know some of them better in a few weeks than I had in twenty years of casual association.

These meetings were a great comfort and inspiration to me. They were the only environment in which I found the warmth of my beloved Chilean people, a warmth that I had very much missed. Everyone greeted one another warmly and seemed to be at home with everyone else. There was an obvious bubbling joy and vitality, a mutual helpfulness regardless of age or economic status that seemed to me like real Christianity come alive again. Service to anyone within or beyond the group was taken for granted. Above all, there was the strong sense of God's presence through the sharing of his revealed word, through the response of individuals praying spontaneously their thanksgiving and praise with simplicity and great sincerity, and through the testimonies of God's work in so many lives.

Six weeks of such meetings with different groups under varying circumstances, plus the instructions given during the meetings and private personal reading made me want to receive the baptism in the Spirit. My one reservation was the gift of tongues for which I not only felt no desire but even repugnance, because of its strangeness and my own timidity about plunging into the unknown. But there was no point to telling God what he should be doing or how he should be doing it. So I finally forced myself to pray, "Lord, I want everything you've got. Please pay no attention to my fears and prejudices."

One evening about this time I went to a private home where some forty people gathered to hear Dr. Maxwell White, a minister from Canada. Dr. White did not hesitate to air his reservations about Catholics and for me personally that did not help matters any. But I tried to listen with a completely open heart. During his talk I suddenly felt a deep and quietly joyous peace come over me. From what I had already heard and read, I took this to be the coming of the Spirit. I also felt that God wanted me to give public testimony to his work in me. So after the talk I congratulated Dr. White on his sermon and asked him to pray over me. We both knelt down, each with one arm around the other, and in the presence of everyone, out loud, he prayed over me. I still felt nothing more than the inner peace. And that continued to be my state in the car going home as those in the car kept praying over me both in English and in tongues. That is the way I went to bed.

But the next morning I woke up feeling, quite unexpectedly, like a different person. I felt rested and relaxed. The inner confusion and sense of frustration were gone. I could concentrate. I felt, in a sense, that the devil was off my back. Prayer was a special joy. I could hardly finish an Our Father for the great desire to linger lovingly over every sweet word and ponder it in my heart. The Mass and each prayer of the Mass took on a whole bright new meaning and vibrant life. Each word penetrated so deeply and came from so deep in my being that I could not but say each word slowly, with great reverence and savor.

After I had prepared my breakfast tray, suddenly, without even thinking about it or in any way willing it, I began to pray in tongues. It was very brief but enough to let me know that it was the real thing. This, I knew, had to be deliberately encouraged for a while. So after lunch I sat down and quite deliberately began praying in tongues as the Lord seemed to give it to me. A beautiful inner peace and joy came over me as I did so. It could only be the Lord's work.

From then on everything clicked and the work projects got under way and were concluded with a speed, depth, and freshness that I could not have anticipated. Scripture came newly alive and was so strongly the living voice of God speaking to me that at times Jesus seemed to spring up alive from the pages of the Gospels. Preaching became a new joy and the appropriate message came easily, with a new spontaneity and force.

At the International Charismatic Conference at Notre Dame in June 1971 I heard Father Michael Scanlan explain the charismatic dimensions and power of the sacrament of Penance. This rang so obviously true that I immediately began administering the sacrament in this new way. The noticeable effects have encouraged me to continue ever since.

In giving retreats, I began to preach the complete message of the New Testament plus the Vatican II teaching on charismatic gifts, devoting the evenings to a long prayer meeting. This group prayer of praise and thanksgiving added to the new approach to the sacrament of Penance have increased greatly the effectiveness of private counseling interviews. Every retreat is full of surprises at the things the Lord is doing, including both interior and exterior healings.

Since my return to missionary work in Chile, I have been given permission to devote time to the charismatic renewal while continuing to be based, at my own suggestion, in a parish. Our work is where people are and they are necessarily localized in their homes within a parish. The Bible-study groups have now become Bible-prayer groups: five adult groups, one mixed adult and youth, and one all youth. All but two meet in homes. Already I have found that people have changed more, and more community spirit has been created, in just the first six months of Bible-prayer experience than in three years of Bible-study meetings. Contrary to all previous parish experience, the groups are now, after a year and a half, able to continue meeting and praying together weekly during the summer without a priest or religious present. Moreover, God has repeatedly shown his presence and power by interior and exterior healings that lead to a continuous deepening of faith and confidence among the people. No two meetings are alike but God is tangibly present and at work in every one of them. The unexpected is always happening, thanks to his hand in everything.

In the transformation of families from sadness and tension to peace and happiness, from wife-beating and gross abuse to respect and concern, from religious alienation to return to God, we see the direct social action of the charismatic renewal. The family is the primal social unit, and without changes in families and in individuals, no change of system or structure will accomplish anything. Without interior change, people will simply use new systems to achieve old and selfish purposes.

Giving charismatic retreats as part of a team and helping different parishes establish their own prayer groups has added a new dimension, a new depth, and a new hope to missionary work, even while we continue our schools and personal attention to the poor. In the schools, Bible-prayer meetings have become part of the formation classes. While visiting the sick in homes and in hospitals, praying over distressed people who come for counseling and praying over babies who are supposed to be under the curse of the "evil eye," I feel a strong urge to pray in tongues.

Happily, a workshop on prayer plus a retreat by Father George Kosicki have created both a climate of understanding and the sympathetic collaboration of Spirit-filled fellow missioners. Satisfying the people's thirst to pray together, mission work has entered into a new age and into a new current that is running strongly throughout God's Church.

Fr. Gerry Ragis / 9

Rev. Gerald R. Ragis was ordained in 1963 in Vermont. He has served as diocesan director of the Cursillo Movement, and is now spiritual director to the IHS Charismatic Community in the Burlington, Vermont area. He teaches religion at Rice Memorial High School in South Burlington, and also has a weekend ministry in St. Francis Xavier Parish where he resides.

Fr. Gerry Ragis

"**I know how much** you trust the Lord...and I feel sure you are still trusting him as much as ever. This being so, I want to remind you to stir into flame the strength and boldness that is in you, that entered into you with the laying on of hands. For the Holy Spirit, God's gift, does not want you to be afraid of people, but to be wise and strong, and to love them and enjoy being with them. If you will stir up this inner power, you will never be afraid to tell others about our Lord."

2 Tim. 1:5-8 (*Reach Out*, Tyndale House)

Through these words of St. Paul to the young priest Timothy the Lord touched my life deeply and led me, gently but surely, into active involvement in the charismatic renewal.

I first came into contact with the charismatic renewal in Vermont one warm August evening in 1970 when some friends invited me to attend a prayer meeting. I had been curious for some time about such gatherings and, frankly, I was rather frightened. The people gathered in a private home in the north end of Burlington. During the first part of the prayer meeting I was quite "up tight" and didn't really know what to expect, but as I gradually began to relax and tried to pray I found that I liked what I was doing. At the end of the evening, without really knowing just what to expect, I asked to be "prayed over."

Nothing really happened to me, and my life went on just the same as before. I had been a priest for seven years, and although I was not satisfied with my prayer life, I covered over any guilty feelings with the rationalization: "My work is my prayer." Aside from celebration of the Eucharist I no longer spent much time in prayer. Yet much of the previous fifteen years had been spent in an attempt at prayer in some form or another. Deep down I did experience an almost nagging hunger for God, a hunger for prayer, for that closer union with the Lord. But in 1970 nothing much was happening.

In September I began my second year teaching in the area high school and, for various defensive reasons, developed a serious case of being turned off to the pentecostal movement. To justify myself I began to talk against those who were praying in that manner. I wasn't praying at the meetings but rather spending my time in magnificent rash judgment: "And what is your problem?" "What's wrong with you?" and so forth.

As chairman of our diocesan liturgical commission I went to Louisville in November to attend the meeting of the National Federation of Diocesan Liturgical Commissions. The Lord used this occasion to work on me. I was still not praying and not happy about my life.

During the opening address in the darkened ballroom a priest came in and sat next to me. There was something vaguely familiar about him but I could not really see him nor his name tag. Every now and then he'd comment to me, "He's leaving out the Holy Spirit . . ." "No mention of the work of the Spirit. . ." I was curious who this guy was. After the talk I met him in the foyer. It was Fr. George

Kosicki. I had only seen George once before, when I heard him talk about biochemistry and the spiritual life. Yet for some reason he remembered me. I had heard that he was working full-time in the renewal. We visited for awhile, then he excused himself to go to pray. My impulse was to ask if I could go and pray with him, but I was scared and didn't.

Later during the convention I heard George on a panel on priestly prayer, and decided that I had to talk to him. I went back to my room and the urging became stronger and stronger. I picked up the phone and called the hotel desk and asked for his room number. "Please God, let him be in!" I got the elevator and hurried to his room and knocked; no answer. My heart sank. I am not a brave person and hesitate to "bother" people, especially people of national prominence. I returned to the elevator, but just as the car arrived, George stepped out the other door. We had our visit. George was very kind, perceptive, and, guided by the Lord, I am sure he said just what I needed to hear.

I began to pray again and delighted in prayer. Oh, don't get me wrong, I was not converted to this "crazy pentecostal stuff," but I was turned on by prayer again and started seriously seeking the Lord. The rest of the fall and winter I continued praying regularly and studying about the charismatic renewal. The best book I found was Fr. Ed O'Connor's book *The Pentecostal Movement in the Catholic Church.* This made sense to me and greatly calmed my fears, particularly about group hysteria, spiritual can-you-top-this-one-ism, and of course the worst problem of all — those who claimed to speak in tongues. I started going to prayer meetings again, off and on.

One morning in early May 1971 I awoke feeling fresh

and rested and quite aware of the Lord. This awareness stayed with me much of the day, even during classes. It was a day filled with expectations, as if something really good were going to happen. In the afternoon I decided that I would attend the prayer meeting that night. I felt that the Lord wanted me to go. I continued rereading Father O'Connor and prayed. I even went to confession, which I hadn't done in some time. I wanted to be open and ready for the grace of God. The priest I confessed to knew of my struggle with the charismatic "thing" and told me: "Jerry, for your penance you go to that prayer meeting and be as open to the Lord as you can."

That night I wasn't gawking around and looking down my judgmental nose at others: I was quietly praying and turned to the Lord. Somewhere along the line I opened the New Testament and for the first time I read that beautiful passage from Paul's letter to Timothy that I quoted at the beginning. The words were alive, almost jumping off the page and hitting me. The Lord really spoke to me, reminding me to stir into flame the strength and boldness that was already in me from the laying on of hands — at Baptism, Confirmation, Ordination, praying with others. The Lord told me to stop being afraid of myself and others, of what people might think of me; he told me to step out boldly in faith. I read the passage aloud to the group. Then I prayed aloud asking for a new filling of the Holy Spirit.

When I returned to the rectory and got into bed I got out O'Connor's book and started to read. I was reading a section where he discusses the various charisms: "The charisms are one of the chief means by which Christ manifests his presence. Where these are not operative, and especially where they are not believed in, one of the main ways of access to Christ's presence is closed off."

I read this and just closed the book and thought a while. Then I very simply made an act of faith: "Okay, Lord, if you work through these charisms, I believe it!" What happened then I can only describe by my experience. I felt literally grabbed or gripped by the Lord. I felt warm all over. I experienced a great desire to love God, to praise him and thank him. The next thing I knew my arms were in the air and I was singing — singing strange sounds and a strange melody! It was like a river unleashed and just pouring out. More important than what was coming out of my mouth was what was going on in my mind and heart. A passage from John's Gospel kept going through my mind: "From out of his heart shall flow rivers of living water."

That night it seemed there was no "turning it off"; anytime I tried to pray in English I could get only a word or two out and then went right back into the tongue. It was a beautiful experience. I guess I went to sleep praying tongues, and woke up in the morning still joyous and praising the Lord.

I found that having at last given in to the Lord in this new way, he overwhelmed me and carried me along. I experienced a joy and peace that I hadn't known in a long time, a deeper love for Scripture, a patience and tolerance in the classroom that even the students remarked. That year I could hardly wait for the feast of Pentecost. How alive those texts were to me then and since! The Scripture has always been important to me but now texts fairly leap off the pages.

The Lord has taught me a lot in the last two or three years and continues to lead me, gently and surely. I have found since being baptized in the Holy Spirit or, if you prefer, since I "stirred up the gift of God, the strength and boldness that is in me," I am not afraid to tell others about our Lord. I find a new power and a new strength, a new peace and confidence that isn't something I've worked up; it is a gift, the gift of a loving Father.

Fr. Edward Scheuerman / 10

Rev. Edward Scheuerman was ordained for the Detroit archdiocese in 1950. After four years as a parish curate, he spent twelve years at Sacred Heart Seminary, working first as a teacher, then as assistant principal, and finally as a counselor. He then became principal of Aquinas High School in Southgate, Michigan, and for the last three years has served as a counselor in Bishop Gallagher High School in Detroit, and as a pastor at St. Martin's Parish. Fr. Scheuerman is also serving his third year as episcopal vicar for the Detroit-Grosse Pointe Vicariate.

Fr. Edward Scheuerman

An opportunity was offered to the priests of the Archdiocese of Detroit for the first time to participate in a summer house-of-prayer during the summer of 1970. I joined a group of eight priests at the Capuchin Retreat House near Washington, Michigan. We spent four full days of each week for seven weeks together. We set our goals, planned our regimen, dialogued, worshipped, prayed, shared meals and recreation. A resource person joined us for part of each week to share theological, scriptural, and prayer insights with us. We had a chance to really enter into a topic, raise questions, explore ideas, test them.

Each day we would meet for morning prayer, meals, and evening prayer. We planned our daily Eucharistic celebrations and had a time for idea-sharing, too. We tried to really explore the realm of prayer and make adaptations to our particular style of ministerial life. Some of us were in parish work, others were teachers in high schools, others were in special kinds of diocesan work.

An important part of the seven-week experience was the weekly excursion most of us in the Washington House made to Gesu Parish in Detroit for the prayer meeting of the charismatic community that met there each Wednesday evening. I had been to one or two meetings of charismatic prayer groups in the years previous, but this time the Spirit really moved in. I attended the weekly "Life in the Spirit Seminar" conducted by Sister Angela Hibbard, and, at the end of six weeks requested and received the baptism of the Spirit.

Being baptized in the Holy Spirit fulfilled and completed the really outstanding experience of a lifetime. Needless to say, I still am the same person I was before this experience with the Lord and my fellow priests. But I have a different orientation to my life, a fuller joy, a deeper confidence, less fear, greater hope, a capacity to tackle more, a more ready acceptance of the inspiration of the Spirit, a more personal relationship with the Lord Jesus, a willingness and a greater aptitude for prayer.

I still have many of the same problems, but less fear of them and the confidence that the Lord Jesus can accomplish in me what I myself cannot do. I take more time and deliberate effort to see that I have my "hour of prayer," and more when possible. Celebrating the Eucharist brings me ever greater joy and peace that I want to share with those who celebrate with me. To join others for shared prayer I regard as a precious opportunity, one even to be sought out. Time spent alone in prayer is time, special time, with the Lord Jesus.

This is a time of growth for me. It is a time in which there is much to do, but with no frenzy or worry. School days I am a high school counselor in a nearby Catholic high school of over 1300 students. Evenings and weekends I am what I call a "consulting pastor." I am a member of a pastoral team of a fine young priest, Fr. Kevin Britt; a deacon on his way to the priesthood, Ron de'Hondt; and four Sisters.

Our pastoral team meets once each week to plan, review, discuss, our weekly and ongoing work in the parish.

We also meet once each week for shared prayer for an hour. Each of us has an area of ministry that we have agreed to carry on according to our gifts and strengths. Our weekly staff meetings and prayer help us to put it all together in perspective and relate ourselves more intimately with the Lord Jesus Christ.

In the spring of '71 I was elected and appointed episcopal vicar by Cardinal Dearden for the Detroit-Grosse Pointe Vicariate. In the time available I try to meet with the clergy of the area each month, as well as other groups that are part of the vicariate operations. I'm just beginning to realize what it means to be a representative of the archbishop in this area of the archdiocese. We've got a long way to go in trying to realize the vision of the Church that came to us from Vatican II and the Synod in 1969. Realizing this, our Vicariate Council voted to have me give more time to the work of the vicariate beginning in July, 1973. I will be leaving my position at the high school, and giving that time to the work of ministering to the parishes, institutions, and people of the vicariate. I believe this is the direction the Spirit of Jesus is leading me.

I still meet each Thursday with two of my fellow priests for an hour of shared prayer. All three of us were part of the 1970 House of Prayer. It is a time of refreshment and renewal, a source of energy and strength and mutual support in the Lord Jesus. Prayer groups are springing up all over the area, some charismatic. Our parish has two groups meeting now in homes, in addition to the pastoral team. The Spirit breathes where he wills. He can accomplish what we cannot. We only have to remove ourselves as obstacles to his breathing. Yes, there are still problems. But today's problem often becames the stepping-stone to tomorrow's joy. It is often just the Lord's way of politely detouring us around an obstacle or making us pause to remember who is "in charge."

There is much still to be done in the Church and in the world. It will be done, but in the Lord's time and in the Lord's way, with us or in spite of us. Praise the Lord Jesus Christ!

Fr. John Randall / 11

Rev. John Randall was ordained in France in 1953 for the diocese of Providence, Rhode Island. After several years of parish work and high school teaching in France, he studied for a doctorate in theology at the University of Louvain, receiving his degree in 1962. Upon his return to Providence in that year, he began teaching at Our Lady of Providence Seminary, and was made spiritual director in 1964. He later served as director of the Providence Cursillo Movement, and is now part of the pastoral team of St. Patrick's parish.

Fr. John Randall

I guess I've really been concerned with renewal in the Church since before my ordination twenty years ago. This concern was heightened by my seminary experience in France where "the eldest daughter of the Church" had become, in the words of Abbé Godin, "mission country." The parish particularly interested me since I was studying to be a diocesan priest, and questions were then being raised in France about the continued viability of the parish. It seemed at one point in these drab circumstances that I had just about lost faith and hope, when the Lord brought me into contact with the writings of Cardinal Suhard, the Mission de France, and especially Abbé Michonneau and his parish in the red suburb of Paris, Saints Peter and Paul. Here was hope, here was life, here was the Spirit of God. Here was a parish that was truly a "missionary community" (original French title of the book translated into English as *Revolution in a City Parish*). I recently reread the book and praised God again for this influence in my life. It gave me a vision, a hope. I saw Sunday after Sunday a parish that was becoming a community, a missionary community reaching out to all the thousands in that neighborhood, a community that was an attractive fire of love, and finally a community that was a "light on the mountain" to all of France. It could be done!

Before being ordained in 1953 the Lord had led me to a real interest in seminary work, almost despite myself. It wasn't so much that I loved the seminary; it was rather that I believed renewal had to start there if parishes were to become like Michonneau's. A sense of community, of teamwork, had to begin with pastors. I recall spending my deacon summer writing a long paper on the seminary as community. Initially it didn't receive much support at the seminary and my interest waned. But a few years later Charles Davis, then editor of the British *Clergy Review*, received it with enthusiasm and published it.

Meantime I was assigned to teaching in a high school and working in a parish. Those were five very happy years. I was working with youth, in whom I saw hope for the future, and the parish was a real home to me. I could have stayed forever, but the gnawing draw of the Spirit to seminary work persisted. I explained this to my bishop and he sent me to Louvain, Belgium, to study for a doctorate in theology in preparation for seminary work. I cried the day I left the parish; it was, up to then, the saddest day of my life.

During those three hard years "away from the action" I concentrated on scriptural studies, always a first love, and did my doctoral dissertation on John 17, Christ's prayer for unity. The point of the thesis was that this was not a prayer for ecumenical unity, as it was then being used, but rather a prayer and a program of Christian community, not unlike the realized version in the early Church (Acts 2 and 4) and in Abbé Michonneau's parish.

God's providence continued to be marvelous in every detail, for shortly upon my return to Rhode Island I was named to be spiritual director of the diocesan seminary in a position of real influence for renewal.

Then came Vatican II and the notion of "the people of God" began to come alive. In 1964 I found all this brought into very practical focus when I started to get very actively involved in the Cursillo Movement. Here were clergy and laity becoming a dynamic community of God's people, with a good method for renewing the whole Church. Eventually I became a diocesan spiritual director and was extending the potential of this movement into my work at the seminary and into high school and college "Search for Christian Maturity" programs. Everywhere there was instant success, a discovery of community, the joy of Easter. One year each class of the seminary had its own community-building "Search" and we wrote and accepted a charter of community responsibility, with a student senate forthcoming.

Summers I got involved in the training of lay apostles, using Cursillo-derived techniques at first, with a particular thrust toward inner city and social involvement. One summer another priest and I shared an apartment in a tough black housing development.

Meantime the Cursillo Movement and the Search were becoming more accepted after much initial fear. The Catholic Youth Organization (CYO) took over the Search and it spread to every city and town in the diocese. Cursillo Ultreyas were launched everywhere and showed great promise. Some parishes had as many as 100 renewed "community-building" cursillistas. I was elected around this time to be a diocesan consultor, and was invited to serve on a couple of national Cursillo Leaders' Workshops in Newark and Hartford. A further prideful moment came when I was elected to membership in the Catholic Biblical Association and invited to address the New England section of this scholarly body on the theme of unity, or rather "community," in John 17.

These were good years, 1962-67, but then something happened. The post-Vatican II thrust began to run out of gas all over, I guess. We worked as hard as ever, in fact harder, but results were diminishing. The hoped-for perseverance and blossoming of cursillistas, seminarians, Searchers, inner city volunteers, just didn't materialize. Bitterness began to set in, disruption in the seminary, a heightened individualism, reaction, polarization. Ultreyas faded out, priests didn't follow through, parishes were not being renewed as communities. Lay apostolate training became more geared on social improvement, people helping themselves.

Then the Lord moved again — and at first I was alarmed and even resentful. At a Cursillo Leaders' Workshop in Shrewsbury, Mass., on St. Patrick's Day, 1967, Ralph Martin and Steve Clark, members of the National Secretariat of the Cursillo Movement, asked me and another priest our opinion on an experience they had just had in Pittsburgh. They recounted a tale of a marvelous revival of charismatic gifts in the power of the Holy Spirit — a rebirth of prophecy, speaking in tongues, and healings. I was horrified, and so was the other spiritual director. We quoted St. John of the Cross to them in warning, and begged them not to bring this into the Cursillo Movement. It was doing OK on its own and, besides that, was in enough "hot water" already with its renewal efforts. All I could think of were "holy rollers" and pietistic aberrations of all sorts in the course of history. I was disillusioned and confused, because Ralph and Steve had given me so much hope prior to that.

One thing the Lord did for me by this experience, however, was to pull my attention to this renewal of the Spirit's outpouring. Articles began to appear in the *National*

Catholic Reporter and *Ave Maria,* etc., and I read all of them I could get my hands on. I knew some of the main characters!

The summer of 1967 saw me plunged just as deeply as ever into inner city and Cursillo work. Then one day in late August, while waiting in the office of the inner city director I noticed on his shelf a book called *The Cross and the Switchblade* by David Wilkerson. I recalled Steve Clark's suggestion that we all read that book and how he had tried to get Mr. Wilkerson to address the National Cursillo Convention the previous summer in New York. I borrowed the book and started reading it that night. I couldn't put it down until I had finished. It was a tremendous grace of the Lord. He was saying to me "Ephphatha, John, be opened." Here was an incredible story of faith, pure gospel faith, in the slums of Brooklyn, where a young minister, armed simply with the Gospel and the power of the Spirit, started a real Christian renewal, and that among the dregs of society! They were so successful they even opened their own kind of seminary or Bible school, while we were having a genuine vocation crisis working with the best of Christians! I gave the book to several associates, especially those working with me on the college scene. To my shame I didn't do much else, however, until a few of us decided in May of 1968 to take a trip to Brooklyn to see this Wilkerson thing.

That Saturday radically changed my life. The reality of Wilkerson's ministry was even more amazing than the book. I remember a former fifteen-year heroin addict who conducted us around that day, now a dynamic Christian apostle. Another kid there had had over twenty-five trips on LSD. At a rally that night Donald Wilkerson, David's brother, spoke on prayer like I had never heard before. We were all moved and asked him to pray for us when the invitation came at the end. I recall him asking me, "Father, what would you like me to pray for?" I said, "I guess I could use some help in my work at the seminary and with lay people." He prayed very beautifully, laying hands gently upon my shoulder, and asked the Spirit to come in power and fulfill that request, renewing my whole ministry. Nothing dramatic happened on the spot, but somehow I believed in his prayer and thanked him.

We got back to Providence about 4 a.m., and I had the eight and nine o'clock Masses that morning in St. Catherine's Church near the seminary. My only thought, honestly, was to somehow get through them and then catch up on some rest. But the Lord had other plans, beautiful ones! I can't explain it yet, but that eight o'clock Mass was something brand new. Everything was ringing, singing: the words, the gestures, the people, especially God! I don't know what I said in the homily, but you can tell when you have an audience in the palm of your hand. That one was. I was sort of scratching my head in bewilderment walking off the altar, wondering what had happened, and then, and only then, did it dawn on me what Wilkerson had prayed for the night before. Maybe, I thought, this is what they meant by the "baptism in the Spirit." The same thing happened at nine o'clock Mass and at every Mass since. Now get me right. I had always loved the Mass, I had experienced many powerful Masses, especially at Cursillos and Searches, but never anything approaching this experience.

Again to my shame I did nothing much with this grace. Once again that summer, I went back to inner city involvement and Cursillo work, and no time was left for the promised extra prayer with that group who had traveled to Brooklyn with me. We were, ironically, too busy doing the

Lord's work. But the "Hound of Heaven" relentlessly pursues. It was so clear that he had a hand on me and that he wasn't going to let me go.

With October came another grace, a new Cursillo Leaders' Workshop. Paul DeCelles, a professor of physics at Notre Dame, was on the team and it became evident to me that he must be involved in this pentecostal renewal. There was something about him that struck right to the heart. So after the weekend was over, back in my room at the seminary I talked with Paul way into the night, listening with fascination to tales from Notre Dame about what the Spirit was doing in the lives of so many people. Around 4 a.m., Fr. Mort Smith of Newark, also on that workshop team, and I knelt down and asked Paul to pray over us for something more of that Spirit. He did. It was the first time I ever heard a Catholic pray in tongues, and I wasn't frightened. It was just so natural, his faith was so great, and he a scientist!

I took Paul to the airport a few hours later and taught class all that morning. Then around noon, without thinking, I picked up my breviary, and it happened again! Like the Mass at St. Catherine's, the office was brand new; the psalms were jumping right out of the book at me. I couldn't get through more than one. The Scriptures became fantastically alive for me — as if a light had gone on. I couldn't get enough of them. I learned more about God's Word in that one moment than I had in years of exegetical study.

From then on I guess you might say I became open to the Spirit, to what he wanted to do; to his power, so amazingly available; to his wisdom, so clear to the eye now. It was a new ball game. I understood what the Lord was now doing in his Church — renewing the whole mystery of

Pentecost, just as he had renewed the mystery of Easter in the previous decade. Pope John's prayer for a renewal of his wonders in our day was being heard. The gas the Church had run out of through human effort was back in supply, and in abundance!

It now became just a matter of time before things mushroomed in Rhode Island. Ralph Martin's sister, Teresa, a student at Salve Regina College in Newport, helped tremendously in getting us launched. A weekly prayer meeting began at the housing project apartment of one of the inner city workers in Pawtucket. It has continued ever since, and grown and grown and grown as the Gospel of "good news" should.

The summer of 1969 saw me in inner city work again, but this time with a new and different approach, proceeding from prayer, the Word of God, and the Spirit. Eleven of us formed a community for the summer in Holy Ghost parish in Providence, and decided to try to rediscover Paul's direct approach of bringing the power of Jesus, and Jesus crucified, to his hungry people. It worked. The word spread. By the end of the summer the parish had a prayer meeting of some 70 people. Come September, the "community" had to break up and return to teaching, to school, jobs, etc. But the Lord continued to work. The prayer meeting continued to grow and grow, until it reached eventually 600 to 700 people, with some 25 to 30 or so other groups branching off that original one and prospering all over southern New England.

In the spring of 1971 it became apparent that I couldn't continue to work in the seminary and also do this work of renewal. Here again the Lord led me. He inspired Fr. Ray Kelly, librarian of the seminary for many years and soon to be named a pastor, to petition the bishop with me to let us try this Christian-community-building approach in an inner city parish. To our pleasant surprise he agreed and we were assigned to St. Patrick's near the state capitol in Providence.

What the Lord wants us to do now, we're convinced, is to let him rebuild a typical parish as an example, a "city on the mountain," to show hope to the whole Church of the Spirit's power to renew. Already in less than two years, the closed school has reopened, people are moving in significant numbers back into a deteriorating neighborhood, hope is coming alive, a community like the one I experienced with Fr. Michonneau at Saints Peter and Paul in Paris is becoming visible. Our dream is a missionary community, an alive people reaching out to all their neighbors until the blaze of Jesus' love reaches every corner. God's plans are so marvelous. I'm persuaded that what he has started he will finish.

Fr. John Madden / 12

Rev. John Madden, C.S.B., entered the Basilian novitiate in 1939. He took a master's degree in English at St. Michael's College, University of Toronto, while preparing for his ordination in 1948. He received his doctoral degree at Harvard University in 1953, and then returned to St. Michael's College where he taught until 1969. During these years, he also served as director of Religious Student Activities (1953-1960), superior of Religious House (1958-1961), and chairman of the English Department (1962-1966). In 1960 to 1962, he was on the board of directors of the National Liturgical Conference, and he has served as member and chairman of the Archdiocese of Toronto Senate of Priests. Fr. Madden is now working in the Houston, Texas area, where he is a member of the advisory committee of the Houston-Galveston Charismatic Community, and is also a member of the Senate of Priests for the Galveston-Houston Diocese.

Fr. John Madden

For the past year, since I was prayed with to be baptized in the Spirit in June of 1972, the Eucharist has had a power in my life I never dreamed possible; my prayer as a newly-ordained priest — that the daily celebration of Mass would always be marked with the faith and fervor of my first Masses — has been answered as only the generosity of God can answer prayer. The Eucharist has truly — not just in theory — become the "summit and source" of my life with the Lord, and with his people.

The sense of God's presence — about which I always loved to preach, rather wistfully — has become a powerful ever-present awareness, as sensible, as real, as the feeling of my body or the temperature of a room.

My eagerness to read God's Word — prayerfully and in love — has given a whole new dimension to my life with the Lord; the readings of the daily Eucharist, the psalms of the office, the daily reading of the Bible are all moments of light and love. The long periods of depression which during my priestly life had paralyzed me — physically, emotionally, and sometimes morally — have given way to an abiding joy and trust in Jesus. Temptations continue — as they must — but I can now face them with the calm and security that comes with the conviction that Jesus has won the victory over sin, and shares it with me in the power of the gifts of his Spirit.

The Lord had graced my life with wonderful friends, and I always treasured their love and concern for me, and tried to see them as occasions for growing in the Lord's love. But somehow the freedom to love — simply, honestly, generously, joyously, freely, fearlessly — and to share the experience of this love, was always fettered by fear: the fear of "feeling" human love, the fear of being misunderstood, the fear that the love might be betrayed, even defiled, by my own weakness. In this past year the Lord has shown me how truly "celibacy frees us for love," and has granted me friendships with those who share this life in the Spirit, and with families and individuals in the parish where I live and in the University where I teach, friendships which have taught me — especially in the selfless love of husbands and wives for one another and for their children — how to love as a priest and as a religious.

But what of my childhood and youth in a truly faith-filled home? What of all I learned and experienced in my years in the religious life and in the priesthood before this renewal of life in the Spirit? I would not want any of it changed — except for my own infidelities to Jesus, my Lord. *All* of it — the religious experiences of a Catholic childhood; the sound theological training of the novitiate; the years of professional education and teaching; the conferences and retreats I have given to laymen, religious, and priests; even, I guess, my own many mistakes — all of this I now see as the preparation for the years, however many or few they may be, that Jesus will give me to live in his Spirit. It is as if a ray of powerful light has been cast on all I ever knew about Jesus, his teaching, and his Church; a power, an eagerness, has been let loose in me to share these riches — to share them in my work in the parish, in my teaching in the University, in the opportunities I now have in abundance to share by preaching and in prayer groups, with all who love to hear how to let Jesus be really their Lord.

The Holy Spirit has offered himself to me, challenged me, enlivened me, freed me. If only I can respond by being all that he wants!

Fr. Francis MacNutt / 13

Rev. Francis S. MacNutt, O.P., is presently the Director of Merton House in St. Louis, Mo. He entered the Dominican order in 1950 with a BA from Harvard and an MFA in theatre from Catholic University of America. After receiving a PhD in theology from the Aquinas Institute of Theology, he commenced teaching homiletics at the Aquinas Institute and Mount St. Bernard diocesan seminary, Dubuque, Iowa. He served as president of the Catholic Homiletic Society (later to become the Christian Preaching Conference), and later as its executive secretary. In 1966 he dedicated his full time to this work and to founding its new journal *Preaching* (now *Preaching Today*). He has written three books on preaching, including *How to Prepare a Sermon* (Ottawa: Novalis, 1970). He currently works full-time preaching and giving workshops on the healing ministry, an apostolate which has resulted in nine trips to Latin America at the invitation of Catholic missionaries.

Fr. Francis MacNutt

It was back in 1966 that I first heard about the pentecostal movement. In some ways it seems that was only a short time ago. But for me it is a lifetime away.

At that time I was president of the Catholic Homiletic Society and editor of its journal, *Preaching*. As part of my professional duties I attended a Speech Association of America convention in Chicago; while there I met for the first time someone who was actively involved in the charismatic renewal. Jo Kimmel was a teacher of speech at Manchester College in Indiana; several Protestant ministers at this convention had mentioned her as someone who had grown very deep in prayer and who was known for having successfully prayed for several healings. What impressed me most about Mrs. Kimmel was her complete naturalness. There didn't seem to be a division between her ordinary life and the life of prayer. Her talk about Jesus and about prayer and healing was as natural as her talk about her teaching and her children. I couldn't help asking myself how many priests and sisters I knew who could talk so easily and unaffectedly about the Lord.

When I questioned her about the results of her prayer for other people, she wasn't self-conscious in describing miracles of healing. When I expressed surprise about all this happening, she said that it was not at all unusual, that there were thousands of people like herself in this country. (At that time I hadn't met any so I was surprised at her statement.)

The next day I called up a priest friend of mine; together we encouraged her to stay over a day after the convention. It gave us another whole day to hear her share her remarkable experiences of the healing ministry; most impressive of all, she described how many things had changed in her life since she had received the baptism of the Spirit. As I heard about these things — familiar from books, yet strange to my experience — I became hungry to know more.

In the coming months, the early part of 1967, I read some of the books then popular among "neo-pentecostals," such as *They Speak in Other Tongues* by John Sherrill. Happily, I was not plagued by the doubts and skepticism that disturb some Catholics, but found myself thirsting to receive the baptism of the Spirit. I have found the same thing true of many Catholic priests; deep down — not in spite of our tradition but because of it — we have really been prepared to understand the baptism of the Spirit and the charismatic gifts. I had learned in my study of spiritual theology that *all* men are called to sanctity, and that sanctity meant a real union with God through the gifts of the Holy Spirit; I had read the lives of the saints and was impressed by the personal knowledge of God they seemed to have experienced in prayer; I knew the accounts of miraculous healings at authentic shrines like Lourdes. Why was it, I wondered, that most of us didn't receive any of these prayer experiences? Why should miracles take place in only a few special places? Why study and read about these things if we were not to expect them?

When I entered the Dominican novitiate in 1950 I was filled with enthusiasm, as most novices are, desiring to devote my full energy to "striving for perfection," as we then put it. My hope was that by giving my entire life to God as best I could something would really happen. I had "left the world" in order to follow Christ; surely this would lead to sanctity. As one pope proclaimed, "Show me a Dominican who has kept his rule and I will canonize him."

Nevertheless, two things in our experience jarred with the ideal. One was that some of the seminarians who were the most serious about striving for perfection seemed to give out in their physical or psychological health. I remember several students whom I had held up as models for myself who suffered nervous breakdowns within a few years and were forced, neither through their own desire nor that of the formation directors, to leave the seminary. They were few in number but what was disturbing was that their decline was not helped but rather occasioned by their strict living according to the model of silence, mortification, and study which they had been given.

My own health, too, began to deteriorate in some ways in spite of the fact that I exercised regularly and took the appointed recreation and sleep. In all my waking hours, I concentrated on prayer and study as we were supposed to do. I also kept the rules that were given to us — silence and so on — as best I could. Under this regimen my weight dropped some twenty pounds in the novitiate year. I eventually realized that I was going to have to slow up in order to continue this race for perfection. In some ways I was happy; I was becoming more self-disciplined; my intellectual abilities were sharpened; but somehow, without being able to put my finger on it, I knew that something was missing.

The second thing that gave cause for reflection was

that we younger members of the order were kept separate from the community's elder members. We were told that these categories were a prudent rule for our own benefit, and that, in the course of time, we would understand the wisdom of the system. What we suspected at the time later turned out to be true: we were kept from associating with older members of the community lest our enthusiasm be dimmed by talking with those whose lives did not strictly accord with the model of perfection we were encouraged to follow. There were great men in our order—men of prayer, men who gave of themselves completely; yet the authorities could not trust that we younger members could safely associate with them, for there were always those whose enthusiasm for preaching and speaking about the things of God had waned; somehow they had found themselves in a kind of spiritual vacuum, a landscape characterized by heaped-up newspapers, TV guides, and empty glasses.

As I grew older and was myself ordained I could readily understand what had happened. It was as if the men had tried for a period of years to live according to an ideal, but had eventually decided that some of it wasn't working for them. They had found themselves in a desert and had stopped at a friendly oasis. Again, it was as if a few people had arrived at a joy-filled union with God, but for most life was a matter of doing a job well, of taking an assignment without complaint. "Well done, good and faithful servant"; but there must be more Good News than what we were seeing in our lives.

After ordination I was appointed to teach homiletics both in the Dominican seminary, The Aquinas Institute, and Mt. St. Bernard diocesan seminary in Dubuque, Iowa. In these years (1958-66), the gap between the ideal and the real became still more apparent; I was now called upon to preach retreats, so I had to preach about the Christian life and *how* to reach that ideal. Not only for myself now, but for others, I had to be realistic and practical in figuring out why when all men were called to contemplative union with God, so few seemed to reach it. Most spiritual authors gave the explanation that most Christians — including many religious — were not generous enough, that they simply gave up carrying the cross. In the search for God there were nights of the soul and deserts to traverse. Somewhere in the various nights of the senses and of the soul the aspiring Christian would lay down his cross and begin hankering for creature comforts. The answer always given was, "Carry your cross generously; and do not seek another one. Keep carrying it, and, eventually, you will be rewarded even if it is not in this life. Above all, do not give up. Be more generous with yourself and you will be all right." For eight years I had accepted this explanation of my failures for myself, but I discovered that when I preached to communities of sisters, many of whom had been striving for years to become holy, I could not tell them they were not generous or that they hadn't carried their cross. That simply didn't seem to be true. If anything they were too generous; they were working too hard. And yet, with good women striving for holiness, there was sometimes unhappiness. How to explain it? How to preach about it? It seemed to me there must be other explanations for what seemed to be missing.

Like many retreat masters of those days, I began to emphasize the other side for balance — encouraging sisters, for example, not to feel guilty about taking needed recreation. We needed balance to counteract a nagging suspicion that if we had not achieved sanctity, it was because we were not really trying hard enough. But that still didn't give the answer: how do we achieve this joy-filled Christian life that the Gospel talks about? And if I was called to preach about it, how would I make the sermon practical? I was also giving retreats and sermons to lay people — especially Third Order groups. Again, the question was insistent: if lay people are also called to sanctity how was I going to preach this in a practical way?

So I kept searching for new ways of preaching. It wasn't just a search for gimmicks; it was a search for content, for reality. To be frank, I really didn't find anything very practical. I had sermons on prayer and sermons on love, but still there was this gap — a gap which I found existed in the lives of most priests and sisters whether they were conscious of it or not. Like many priests of that time (the early '60s), I began to look for practical assistance from the field of psychology. I began to read Carl Rogers, Abraham Maslow, and especially Erich Fromm, and gained many insights and practical suggestions in relation to counseling and the nature of love. If the core of Christian life consists of love then a vital question is, "How do we live this life of Christian love?" The books written by Rogers and Fromm contained valuable insights. When you got right down to it, they seemed more practical than most of the devotional books on Christian love that I had read.

As a result of my desire to meet the needs of retreatants I found myself injecting more and more psychology into my sermons and retreats. Finally I developed a weekend retreat which was entirely on the subject of Christian love. I was aware that the only talk that could be termed explicitly Christian was the very first one that spoke of

Jesus' command that we love one another as we love ourselves and, beyond that, as he had loved us. The rest of the retreat was based on practical suggestions discovered through group dynamics and psychology and a lab on how to live in community and communicate with one another.

These retreats seemed to be highly successful. At the end of some of our high school retreats the students simply didn't want to go home. They found the old cliques breaking down, animosities and hatreds healed by the spirit of love engendered in the group. This seemed to be a great improvement over the old style retreat in which the retreat master stood up to speak to a captive audience in the high school gymnasium.

I realized that we had come up with something new and good in retreat format and content — something that was working. And yet, at the same time, I realized that my basic source of inspiration was not the Gospel, but psychology. I could have left out the one explicitly Christian talk without harming the retreat too much. My retreat could perhaps have been put on still more successfully by trained group dynamics experts. (Later, in fact, our young priests did get professional training in group work.)

While I wondered about this, many other priests in my situation were asking similar questions. Were we simply becoming counselors? Or mathematics teachers? Were priests fulfilling a variety of functions that could be just as well performed by someone else? If we had PhDs in counseling or psychology could we do a better job than we had been doing? The answer seemed to be yes. But if so, did a man need to be a priest to carry on the work that was actually most beneficial to people? About that time many of my best friends in the order left. Some had come to identify themselves primarily as teachers or counselors; aside from the loss of celebrating Mass they felt that they could be more effective in their work somewhere else than in our community. And these were not misfits; some of them were our best men. And so I was forced to ponder not simply the matter of effective preaching, but the roots of everything: what does it mean to be a Christian; in light of that, what does it mean to be a priest? I was personally not strongly tempted to give up the active ministry of the priesthood, but I understood the agonizing questions so many of my fellow faculty members were asking.

My experience as a counselor and confessor also prepared me to understand the charismatic renewal. I had found that, aside from the sacramental aspect, the real help I was able to give people came mostly through my being willing to listen and to care for and about them as best I could. I worked in conjunction with psychiatrists who referred their patients to me for spiritual direction, but there were just too many people needing help. I couldn't take on more than about ten; even that was interfering with my class preparation. Yet they desperately needed the help of a counselor. And why was it that those people who were hurting the most seemed to be the ones no one, neither the psychiatrist nor anyone else, could really help? If Christianity is the good news of being saved, why do some people have a head start, while others seem to be helpless from the very beginning? The more I studied psychology the more I realized how much was determined in people's lives before they reached the use of reason; some people were so deeply hurt by rejection in their childhood that they were likely to be damaged for life. To such a person the Good News did not seem to be good news, no matter how much I preached about it. They would say, "Well, God may love you, but he certainly doesn't seem to love me. Look at me. I am the living proof." Some would explicitly ask, "You do think that I'm hopeless, don't you, Father? I'm never going to be better." Deep down I would think to myself, "I can't say that they are hopeless, but humanly speaking, they certainly are." At that time, at least six of the people referred to me for counseling had either contemplated suicide or had actually attempted it. So I couldn't help asking myself, "Why is it that the people I can help as a priest are the relatively normal people while the people that are suffering the most interiorly are the very ones that no one seems to reach?" It was as if there was a determinism in the universe which seemed to conflict with the message of Jesus: that he had come to proclaim release to captives, to help the lame to walk. He came to the poorest of the poor, the outcasts — the prostitutes, the tax collectors. Those were the people that Jesus loved. It was as if a power was in Jesus that was missing in my life. At the time it didn't surprise me that I couldn't do the works that Jesus did — even though he said, "I tell you most solemnly, whoever believes in me will perform the same works as I do myself, he will perform even greater works. . ." (John 14:12). All these things left me with a vague, but real, sense that something was missing. And I had a sense of urgency to find out the answers if there were any — a sense of urgency arising from my best friends' leaving, as well as from my desire to find the depth needed to preach the Gospel. There was an added urgency in the lives of the psychologically wounded that I was directing. Were they hopeless humanly speaking? If so what is the reality of Christ's saving message? Is the priest nothing more than a referral service to the psychiatrist and social worker? Did I have good news to offer the sick, as Jesus did — the good news of healing? Or was I merely confined to good advice?

That was why, in 1966, when I heard that there were people who prayed for healing it made a great deal of sense to me. Maybe this was what was missing in my life that would put everything together. I was determined to investigate the baptism of the Spirit, even though, at that time, I had heard of no Catholics who knew about this phenomenon. I had, of course, the usual problems that a Catholic would have, especially at a time when nothing was written that would build the bridge I needed. I had the usual questions: what is this baptism of the Spirit, assuming that I have already received the Spirit in baptism, confirmation, and ordination? And yet, in the people I met who claimed to have been baptized in the Spirit, I saw the fruits of the Spirit: love, joy, and peace. It radiated in their eyes. They were speaking of an experience which I could not contradict; nor did I want to, because it seemed to hold such great hope of what was missing in our lives. Had not the spiritual writers said that union with God could only come as a gift? And to receive a gift, we need only ask, rather than strive to achieve it on our own. These people I met were speaking of their experiences of gifts of the Spirit — the same gifts I could identify by name, having read about them in the theological works of Garrigou-Lagrange. As they would describe some experience I could almost see the page on which I had read about such things either in the abstract or in the life of some saint. Here were Protestants who surprisingly seemed to be living the ideals that we professed in religious life. For instance, in our Dominican rule it was set down at the very beginning that we should be like St. Dominic who either spoke to God or about God. Here I had discovered Protestant friends living out that ideal which had seemed too literal for many of us; they were doing it without any particular rules or blueprints. Led by an interior movement of the Spirit, they seemed to want to talk about God — or pray to him. They were talking, not about the historical Jesus from a book, but about a friend. I saw no divergence between the ideal that I had always held as a Catholic and the experiences of these, my Protestant friends.

The following summer, August, 1967, Mrs. Kimmel made it possible for me to attend a kind of mammoth retreat called a "Camp Farthest Out" (CFO) in Maryville, Tennessee. I went to this Camp with the hope of receiving the baptism of the Spirit, whatever that might mean for me. When I arrived I was surprised to find that there were 800 people at this Camp spending six days in a format very much like a traditional Catholic retreat — three sermons a day with prayer interspersed and a lot of lively discussions. I did find differences, not in the format, but in the experience of the people.

What struck me as a teacher of homiletics was that all three speakers spoke for at least an hour (including Rev. Tommy Tyson, Mrs. Agnes Sanford, and Rev. Derek Prince) and yet the audience did not grow tired of listening to them; in fact the entire group seemed ready to listen for another hour. I realized that I was hearing the gift of inspired preaching which I had talked about in my homiletics courses. I remembered that one of the traditional signs of predestination given by St. Thomas Aquinas was that a person would *gladly* listen to the Word of God — something we had not always seen in our own parishes where people were glad for a short sermon. I remembered those closings of Forty Hours (in the days we had them) when the pastor would caution me in the sacristy, "You know, we appreciate short sermons here." And so you wouldn't miss the point, several of the men would be reading their breviaries while you spoke.

Another thing that impressed me was that the people were talking about Jesus and about their experiences of God in a most natural way. In our retreats we had had a rule of silence, so that retreatants would not be distracted by talk. But here was talk that was not a distraction, because there were people who had an inner desire, whether there were rules or not, to talk about the things of God. Again, this was in accord with our spiritual tradition in which "virtue" by definition brings about a *desire from within* to do those things gladly that the law can only impose from without. Here were people living according to the deepest virtue, according to grace. We had been trying for so long to impose those same ideals through law.

Not being sure theologically what the baptism of the Spirit was or how it was related to the sacraments, I knew enough about its effects upon people to decide that I wanted it. Even if it meant feeling like a fool I would have to take the plunge in the midst of all these Protestant people, only two of whom I knew. So I made an appointment to pray in a small group for the baptism of the Spirit, with the company of four other people. This small group prayed with great fervor for us, but, although I felt good about the prayer, nothing special happened. This particular group stressed tongues strongly — so much so, that if you hadn't spoken in tongues, they would not believe that you had received the Spirit. Therefore, they asked me if I would like to pray in tongues, and I said,

"Yes." So I did — very fluently in something that sounded like Russian.

Nevertheless, I was still disappointed because I was not looking for a particular gift but for a deeper experience of Christ which I knew was at the center of it all. I was frustrated and confused as these prayer group leaders were congratulating me and telling me I had received the Spirit. In the midst of this confusion I had the chance of talking to one of the speakers of that CFO, Mrs. Agnes Sanford, an Anglican who understands the Roman Catholic tradition. She asked how my prayer for the baptism of the Spirit had gone. When I told her of my disappointment she said, "Well, frankly, I had the feeling from the very beginning that this group should not pray for you exactly in the same way they usually do: that you should receive the Spirit, as if it were for the first time. I think it would be better to pray for you for an unfolding of the gifts of the Spirit — a releasing of those gifts that are already within you through baptism and ordination." That made a lot of sense to me.

And so, the next evening, after supper, Mrs. Sanford and two friends prayed for me that I might receive this unfolding of the Spirit, and the release of all his gifts. As she prayed, she also shared a prophecy concerning my ministry as a priest, a beautiful prophecy about how the Lord would work through me in healing and in the sacraments (especially in penance) — and in helping other Catholics, especially priests. As she finished the prayer all four of us were overcome by a wave of laughter. It was just as if a spring of joy had welled up from within me, the joy of the Holy Spirit. Wave upon wave of joy engulfed us. We all laughed together, not hysterically, but because we were filled with the joy of the presence of God. It was in this way — a way that seemed just right and suited for me — that I experienced the baptism of the Spirit. It came in a way that I had not exactly planned, but, rather, in a way that I believe God himself chose and arranged.* Providentially, Mrs. Sanford was there to know how to pray with me. Through her ministry I was to understand what was happening, and through that understanding, to help hundreds of other priests receive the baptism of the Spirit.

For so many of us the Spirit has been there all the time, but quenched or bottled up. The baptism of the Spirit is like a releasing of the Spirit. I have found since then, in praying for many priests, that ordinarily the baptism of the Spirit is for them a very peaceful experience. For some it is overwhelming and a manifest change takes place immediately, but perhaps for most priests the change is gradual and occurs mainly in the area of their ministry. I found, too, that those priests who do not seem to be able to receive any manifest experience of the Spirit are often those who are bound by inner sorrow or hurt. Others have grown used to such a restrained, disciplined manner of life that they are not completely free to respond to the Spirit in all the ways he would desire to express himself, his love and power, in our lives.

The change that this has meant in my own life has been tremendous. As one of the first priests in the Catholic

---

*This same incident is described by Mrs. Sanford in her recent autobiography *Sealed Orders* (Logos). The prophecy has certainly been fulfilled, and priests like Fr. Michael Scanlan, T.O.R., have carried on this work still farther. His book *Power in Penance* (Ave Maria) relates healing to penance.

pentecostal renewal, I found that I was called upon many times to speak to people who had just heard about this movement and were skeptical. The increasing number of requests for talks and retreats that came in forced me to make a choice between my work as executive secretary of the Christian Preaching Conference and editor of *Preaching*, posts which carried a certain amount of recognition and esteem, and a St. Paul type of existence: wandering around and preaching wherever there was a need. I made the decision to launch out; in 1969 I resigned as executive secretary, and in 1970, my editorship. Now that I am released for full-time travel, giving retreats, and praying with people, I feel that I am more at the heart of the Church than ever before; and certainly I feel that I am as close to the Dominican ideal as possible. I find that the gifts of the Holy Spirit manifest in my life simply intensify the work I was already doing in preaching and counseling.

There is a new force to my preaching. I find that I can now speak for an hour without tiring, frequently without notes, and that people want to hear what I have to say about Jesus and the Spirit. The total time of talks given on a weekend retreat back in 1964 would have been about three hours. Today we usually need a team to meet the demands, and the talks, discussions, and group prayer amount to at least twelve hours.

Above all, my work in counseling has changed. Because I have become aware of the power of prayer for healing, I am now able to help those very people whom I thought were hopeless, humanly speaking, back in the 1960s. Through the power of prayer real miracles of healing take place, physical healings, but above all, spiritual and psychological ones. Problems that have a poor psychological prognosis, such as homosexuality, can be cured through prayer. Instant cures of alcoholism and drug addiction are a common occurence.

In recent years I've been called upon to give many institutes on healing for priests. We rejoice to find other priests beginning to understand the healing ministry, which should be a part of their priesthood. The former headquarters of the Christian Preaching Conference in St. Louis has now become Merton House, a center dedicated to reconciliation, a place from which to spread the good news of God's healing ministry. A small team of dedicated workers has gathered to pray with the sick and to give prayer support to the retreats that take us as far as Peru, Bolivia, and Chile, where we share what we have learned about the Good News with our missionaries who have so much to teach us in return. We have experienced the joy of seeing the lives of priests completely renewed and transformed. Those things I had once regarded as a great, but impossible ideal I now see as a matter of course. Typical of the letters we frequently receive is the following:

Dear Father,

Yesterday I was going to write thanking you for giving the greater part of a day to Sister_____ but this morning I can't find words adequate — Sister wrote me and for the first time in four years she is *alive!* After suffering so helplessly and so long with her I can scarcely contain my joy this morning. God has brought about a transformation.

It is seeing lives transformed through Christ working in our ministry that gives us "a reason for the hope that is within" (1 Peter 3:15): for God's people, the Church — and for their priests. All of us who have experienced this transforming power of Christ can say that for us the

Gospel and preaching the Gospel message has changed. It used to be like giving good advice.

But now it means proclaiming Good News.

An Open Letter to Priests

From Bishop Joseph McKinney

My brother priests,

"Jesus Christ is Lord" has become the central theme of my life since August, 1970. It happened when 13 of us priests came together in a secluded cabin in the woods. We decided to make a "prayer" retreat. While we did not know what it would lead to, we decided that we should come together for prayer. Little did we realize that we would experience the power of Pentecost. We asked Father George Kosicki to lead us. He was the instrument for a profound spiritual experience. I found the answer to a key question and a direction for the development of the spiritual life that has enriched my life ever since.

The key question was a challenge that came from a layman. In summary he said, "Bishop, I go to church every Sunday and I hear a different message each time. I am having trouble putting it all together. What the Church needs is a theme! If you give me the theme of the Church, I'll package it for you." This was a solid Catholic family man from New York. He works on Fifth Avenue and is the man who developed the Pepsi ad, "You've got a lot to live, and Pepsi's got a lot to give."

I started my search for the theme of the Church. I had already learned from a study of Saint Paul that the answer had to be in the mystery of Jesus Christ. For seven months I read, questioned, wondered, and looked. What is the theme of the Church? I went to a week-long theological workshop on Jesus Christ but I did not find the answer there. It came in prayer. It came from a man who discovered it while praying the Scripture. The theme is: Jesus Christ is Lord!

Those are the words from an ancient hymn of the Church recorded in the second chapter of Philippians. We find traces of it throughout the New Testament and the whole history of the Church. Fr. Kosicki has continued to develop it. A balanced view of the mystery of Christ includes the three different themes: the Jesus Theme, The Christ Theme, The Lord Theme.

The Jesus Theme: the name Jesus means "God is saving." Here we tie in all of salvation history which finds its climax in the Incarnation and Paschal Mystery. God saves man and man must cooperate to be part of that saving action. We can be liberated from sin and death. Books have been written about salvation history but the words that ring through it are "believe" and "repent." In prayer it means to me that I must include the words "I am sorry" and "I am ready to empty myself." He must increase and I must decrease.

This sets the stage for The Christ Theme. "The Christ" means "the anointed one." It can be shown from Scripture that Jesus was anointed with the Holy Spirit, led by the Holy Spirit, and handed the Holy Spirit over to his followers. The theology of the Holy Spirit as expressed in the Acts of the Apostles and Saint Paul is very moving and dynamic. The words that say the most to me in my experience are "enlighten," "empower," and "enliven." Again we must cooperate. Mary's "Fiat" is a splendid example. We must keep saying yes. This presumes that we are willing to listen and to adjust as God requires.

Once we become instruments of the Holy Spirit, we can live The Lord Theme. "The Lord" brings to mind "Kingdom." In Christ, the Father is forming a community, establishing the pilgrim people of God, and building up the Body of Christ, the Church. Here the sacraments play a key role. All this new creation is pointed toward the Father. The Lord is establishing the Kingdom of God through a servant love. Our response is to be like the self-sacrificing servant love of our Brother, who is the Lord. I must learn to love and serve the real Church, the people of God, as they are, wrinkles and all.

This brief summary can be expanded in many ways. I find this theology expressed in well-balanced prayer communities. Association with them has meant that the Holy Spirit plays an ever-increasing role in my life. When decisions are difficult, I turn to prayer with the conviction that the Holy Spirit will enlighten me. When hearts have to change and challenges cause fear, I turn to prayer with the confidence that the Holy Spirit will supply the power if I am ready to make the adjustments that an honest yes to the will of God demands. When I find myself discouraged or restless, or inclined to bitterness, I turn to prayer with the assurance that the Holy Spirit will enliven me with joy, peace, and love. He comes through whenever the goal is to build up the Kingdom of God. That prayer always seems to be more powerful when I pray with others. Examples are numerous, but my greatest joy has come when I witnessed the power of prayer in working with priests who are struggling with alcoholism.

I have been privileged to be Christ's instrument in a few retreats with priests and seminarians. Often there is a type of polarization over issues that challenge the Church. Not the least of these is the authority crisis in our day. Many priests are troubled; some feel discouraged; most are men of deep faith with a special love for the Church. Priests that leave the ministry are a cause of profound sadness. When the mystery of Jesus Christ is presented, wonderful fruits are harvested. The community is strengthened, and Jesus Christ becomes the key reality. I continue to be amazed at what the Holy Spirit can do if we are willing to be his instruments.

I find that the challenges of life in the Church today are bringing many priests to their knees. Prayer-life is intensified and the spiritual quality of priests, who hang in here in spite of the odds, is deepening. The prayer-forms of the charismatic renewal are difficult for priests because we have been programmed differently. Prayer is seen as a very personal aspect of life and years of effort at personal prayer make open, spontaneous prayer very difficult. Still I have yet to meet a priest who does not want to be a man of prayer. Few are the priests who feel adequate to the task of leading a prayer community. The only answer I know is an increased devotion to the Holy Spirit.

In my mind we need a job description of the role that priests should play in the charismatic renewal. This would include an appreciation of the pastoral gift to discern, admonish, and teach. While many priests find the answer to their own struggle in moments of faith-crisis within the charismatic renewal, they should not play a leadership role until they have integrated their personal faith life and their life as leader of the faith community. A priest with "hang-ups" can cause great harm if he imposes them on the prayer community. When a well-balanced priest takes an active part in a prayer community and has the courage to exercise the pastoral gift, great strides are made in renewal. When we cooperate with the Holy Spirit, awesome power is involved and I suspect that many of us are just starting to recognize that fact.

I might add that the most fruitful days of my priesthood occur when I tithe time to prayer. I decided that two hours and twenty minutes of each day belong to the Lord in prayer. This includes Mass, reading Scripture, time spent alone, and odd moments throughout the busy day. Often we hide behind not having the time, but the truth is that we cannot afford not to find the time. We often play games looking for solutions in the wrong places. Many of today's solutions are off the mark. Their effectiveness is limited. We must abide in him and he abides in us. Prayer is the best means to flesh out the conviction that Jesus Christ is Lord.

Praise the Lord!

**Most Reverend Joseph C. McKinney,
Auxiliary Bishop of Grand Rapids**